The Canadian Cowboy

BY ANDY RUSSELL

Grizzly Country
Horns in the High Country
The Rockies
The High West
Memoirs of a Mountain Man
Andy Russell's Adventures with Wild Animals
The Life of a River
The Canadian Cowboy

The Canadian Cowboy

Stories of Cows, Cowboys, and Cayuses

Andy Russell

with illustrations by
Don Brestler

M&S

Canadian Cataloguing in Publication Data

Russell, Andy, 1915-
The Canadian cowboy : stories of cows, cowboys, and
cayuses

ISBN 0-7710-7880-3
1. Cowboys – Canada, Western – History. 2. Ranchers
– Canada, Western – History. 3. Ranch Life – Canada,
Western – History. I. Title.

FC3209.R3R8 1993 971.2 C93-094788-6
F1060.R8 1993

The excerpt in Chapter 1 is from *Trails Plowed Under* by
Charles M. Russell. Copyright 1927 by Doubleday, a
division of Bantam Doubleday Dell Publishing Group,
Inc. Used by permission of Doubleday, a division of
Bantam Doubleday Dell Publishing Group, Inc.

The publishers acknowledge the support of the
Canada Council and the Ontario Arts Council
for their publishing program.

Typeset by M&S

The support of the Government of Ontario through
the Ministry of Culture, Tourism and
Recreation is acknowledged.

McClelland & Stewart Inc.
The Canadian Publishers
481 University Avenue
Toronto, Ontario
M5G 2E9

1 2 3 4 5 97 96 95 94 93

To all the old cowboys

Contents

Introduction

It all began in 1492 when Columbus sailed into the Caribbean on his first exploration voyage in the service of Spain.
When Cortes, the Spanish conquistador, came to take up
land in Cuba a few years later, he brought horses with him,
for a military officer of his rank without a horse to carry him
and his armour would have been quite unprepared for his
ambitious undertaking: the conquering of huge tracts of land
and the creation of a vast empire called New Spain. In 1521,
two years after Cortes began the Conquest of Mexico, one
Gregario de Villalobos sailed across the Atlantic from Santa
Domingo with a number of calves, "so that there might be
cattle, he being the first to bring them to New Spain." Little
could he realize what an enormous impact his cattle would
eventually exert on the history of North America.

The native Indians, so called because Columbus thought
at first that he had arrived on the coast of India, not realizing
that a continent and the vastness of the Pacific Ocean still
separated him from the Orient, were designated in the

records of the Catholic priests accompanying these first expeditions as animals, even though they walked like men and looked like them. The Spaniards used the Indians to control their growing herds of livestock. The soldiers, of course, paired with Indian women, who, naturally enough, had their babies – graceful crossbred youngsters who grew up on horseback and proceeded to become very skilful horsemen, handling cattle better than their fathers. The priests were somewhat troubled, because these offspring, the get of animals, could not be baptized. They solved the problem by reversing their original classification of "animals" to "men." These children grew up to become the *vaqueros*, "the mounted workers with cows."

In 1540, Coronado took horses, cattle, hogs, sheep, and goats with him on his long expedition in search of the mystical Seven Cities of Cibola. These were the first domestic livestock to enter what is now the United States. Just across the Rio Grande River in New Mexico territory, he abandoned the emaciated and sorefooted survivors of the cattle. Twenty-five years later another Spanish explorer following Coronado's trail found thousands of wild cattle competing with the buffalo, deer, and antelope there.

It was even earlier, in 1528, when the first cattle arrived in Texas, brought there by Cabeza Vaca. By that time the untamed and quarrelsome Comanche, Apache, and Lipan tribes were mounted on horses and did not welcome the intruders, so not much of Texas was settled by the Mexicans for a century and a half. But a Catholic mission was established in 1690 on what is now the border between Texas and Louisiana, just north of the coast, and it was stocked with two hundred cattle. According to the records left in the journals of the priests, this expedition "left a bull and a cow and a stallion and a mare at each of the various rivers crossed" on the way, which may partly account for the thousands of horses and cattle that subsequently roamed Mexico and Texas inland from the Gulf coast. Some of these wore the brands of various missions, but the nature of the land, with its great thickets of scrub trees, arroyos, and the general rough geography, along with the easygoing temperament of the Mexicans working for the missions, gave plenty of opportunity for livestock to run wild. Hunting wild cattle for sport was a popular pastime, though it only eliminated the slower ones, so that the survivors were not only the fleetest but the smartest. The calves they bred inherited all the speed and cunning of truly wild animals.

So it was that the longhorn cattle evolved in a comparatively short time from the basic stock of three distinct breeds originally brought over from Spain. One was the Berrenda, with a white body and black markings around the neck and ears. Another was the Retinto, with a long narrow head and colour ranging from a jersey tan to cherry red. The third was the solid black Andalusian fighting breed. The resulting mix of these three strains of bloodiness was the longhorn, with colours ranging through solid black to red and white and all the variations in between.

Ownership of cattle and the registry of brands identifying them was something that had been done in Britain as far back as Roman times. It involved stamping various identification marks on the hides of calves or mature stock with a hot iron, a practical operation that is still used across the cattle country of North America and has never been improved upon, though freezing and the application of acid have been tried.

In 1529, the town council of Mexico City ordered the establishment of a local stockmen's organization, called the Mesta, the first of all organized stockmen's groups in the western hemisphere. In the same year the council set up a system of registering brands, a system that is now universal. Registered brands were written in a book with the names of the various owners so that the judges, who were required to settle disputes involving strays in various herds, could refer to it. These judges were the first of the thousands of men to be employed as stock inspectors since that time through Mexico, the United States, and Canada.

The longhorn was a big rangy animal with a spread of horns that could on occasion reach more than six feet. It was about as wild as any animal can get. The Mexicans had in their blood the traditional sport of fighting bulls, with all its classical manoeuvres involving the manipulation of a cape and other moves, culminating in the final death of the animal with the thrust of a sword. But it would have taken a very reckless matador indeed to have tackled a wild longhorn bull in a closed arena. The Mexicans did fight them from horseback and they also arranged matches between bulls, longhorns and buffalo, and even longhorns and grizzly bears. Death was the inevitable end of such fights for both animals, for it was easier to kill the winner than turn him loose. The longhorn was a very dangerous animal and killed many men and their horses with its deadly horns.

Meanwhile, the introduction of cattle to new country continued over the centuries. In 1749, Jose de Galvez took cattle with him on a long drive northwest, which crossed the Colorado River at the delta on the northern end of the Gulf of California and proceeded westward to the coast, where it met a ship that had sailed around the Horn on the southern tip of South America. He then trailed his expedition north following the ship to Monteray Bay, where he established two missions. Thus cattle and horses arrived in California along with the first settlement of Europeans.

American settlers from the northern States and those to the south began trickling into the vast expanse of Texas, where they took up farms in what was then Mexican territory and became acquainted with longhorns and cayuses – the small wiry horses descended from Spanish barbs, a breed remarkable for its speed, endurance, and docility. History was moving fast then, and there were skirmishes with the Mexicans as Texas was on its way to becoming a part of the United States. And in due process of opportunity and endeavour, American farmers became stockmen involved heavily with longhorn cattle. When the Civil War burst into flame, many of these tough, singleminded frontiersmen volunteered for service in the newly formed Confederate Army to fight for the south against the military of the northern states.

Riding their tough cayuses that looked like the wrath of God compared to the thoroughbreds of the grey-clad southern gentlemen, these frontiersmen-soldiers not only kept up but distinguished themselves in battle. In what was one of the bloodiest wars in military history, thousands of men on both sides fell, countless numbers to be buried in unmarked graves. When it was over, surviving Texans made their way back to Texas, many of them to find their homesteads burned and their families either killed or driven to the settlements by Comanches and Apaches as well as by white raiders taking advantage of the war to plunder.

Back in Texas during the Civil War almost every man of military age was in the southern Confederate army, which meant that the only help that many of the cattle ranches had were older men, young boys, blacks, and Mexicans. They dressed in buckskin pants and hunting shirts and moccasins, for few of the settlers could have afforded storebought clothes had they even been available. They were armed with flintlock muzzle-loading rifles and pistols, though some acquired percussion five-shot Colt revolvers of .36 and .44 calibre and percussion rifles. The single-shot weapons were no advantage when fighting raiding Indians, for the warriors armed with bows carried many arrows and could handle them fast and accurately. Boys as young as ten to thirteen years old were not only required to do a man's work while handling cattle and horses but also learned to fight with their weapons as soon as they were old enough to carry and load them. It was a rough and most effective frontier school where survivors grew into men who had long since come to terms with fear and pain, men who accepted violence when faced with it and dealt with it effectively to stay alive.

There was drought so severe that during the summer of 1863 when it was at its worst it killed off thousands of cattle. Then during the winter of 1863-64 a series of bad storms from the north swept south to the coastal plains along the Gulf of Mexico. These were dry storms, but so cold that even part of Galveston Bay froze over and more cattle died. This vicious weather caused cattle from further north to drift south with it in many thousands. Still more cattle died. The drought broke when spring came with rains that filled the rivers. The grass came back in abundance and once more the country was green.

It was by this natural process of survival of the fittest that the Texas longhorns became as tough a breed of cattle as ever walked the earth. By the time the war was over and the men came back to Texas to once again take charge of their herds, the cattle were thriving and wandering free in many thousands, many of them unbranded and wild as hawks.

By the same token surviving Texans were anything but soft, for the great majority of them had endured privation, danger, and violence to a degree far beyond most present-day experience. So when they undertook to gather their cattle and add to them with wild ones caught and branded with their brands and then find a market for them, they were ready for anything they might encounter – weather and hostile Indians included. Those cowboys, who were mere boys when they began to do men's work and help defend their homesteads against outlaw raiders and hostile Indians, were graduates of a very tough school of hard knocks, very gentle and soft-spoken by nature for the most part, but highly skilled, and ruthless when conditions called for it.

It was a time of heartache, but it was also a time of opportunity, for the whole of southeast Texas, particularly in the brush-covered breaks to the north of the Rio Grande, was teeming with unbranded cattle waiting to be caught. Hunting wild cattle was no job for sissies, particularly in the breaks along the Rio Grande with the cattle hiding like whitetail deer in the scrub oak and thorn brush thickets. It was done by whatever means the circumstances of geography and the moment called for.

One way was to build a sturdy corral around a waterhole where the cattle came to drink. This was generally done by digging a trench and planting posts close together. Trap gates were used, which were activated by a rope and weights, to be triggered by a well-hidden man, usually up in a tree. Wild longhorns could go for days without water and were very crafty, so the cow hunters had to be extremely careful and patient. It was necessary to leave such a trap corral alone until animals became accustomed to going into it to drink. Even then if a man got on the upwind side of them as they came in for a drink, they would stampede. Some old unbranded range bulls were the worst. Wary as wolves and dangerous as rogue grizzly bears, some of them would attack a rider on sight, sometimes with disastrous results. For instance, two cowboys were up in a tree ready to jerk the line that would trip the gate of a trap to catch a small herd running with such a bull, when all hell broke loose back where they had tied their horses some distance away. It was at night and they waited till daylight before they ventured near where their horses had been left. Both were dead, killed by an outlaw herd bull.

When a herd was trapped, tame oxen were generally employed to take the wild ones, one at a time, to a stout holding pen, where the unbranded ones were branded and the young bulls castrated. One end of a yoke was fastened to a trained ox's neck, and the other end of it was lashed across the wild one's horns. Then the ox patiently took the captive to the holding pen, an operation that sometimes took a long time and sometimes the wild one would kill itself fighting to get free. Branded cattle in a captured bunch could generally be driven with such an ox to lead them.

Another way to capture wild cattle was to sneak up close to them, ride hell-for-leather after them, and rope them. A good rope horse had to be fast, tough and surefooted as a goat, and, like a hunting dog, it purely loved the chase. It was no picnic sitting on such a horse when the chase went through thickets of scrub oak, for the branches are about as ungiving as iron, so a rider had to be good at dodging, flattening out over his horse's neck and weaving from one side of his saddle to the other as the horse ran after a cow flat-out. The rider generally had trouble figuring out what part of him hurt the most after a few days of this kind of work, for there was no way he could dodge everything that came at him.

It was here that cowboys tied their ropes hard and fast to the saddle-horn. They used short ropes, generally not over thirty feet long, and they threw a loop just big enough to go over a cow's head. When they made a catch it was up to the horse. Every rider carried up to half a dozen short lengths of rope. In the timber, they would ride around a tree and pull the animal up close to it, then dismount and tie it to the tree by the horns with one of the tie-ropes, where an ox could be brought to it.

Out in an open meadow, a cowboy would make his throw, pull the slack out of his rope as his horse ran up alongside it, and flip the rope over the cow's opposite side. Then his horse would run off to the side, and when the weight of the animal hit the end of the rope, it went up in the air, made a turn, and came down hard enough to knock its wind out. Before it could get up, the cowboy would take a tie-rope and securely lash three of its feet together, rendering it helpless. Then he could take a tie-rope and tie a front leg to a hind one – a method called side-hobbling. Thus tied and back on its feet an animal would travel, but very slowly.

The California *vaqueros* simplified this manoeuvre by riding up alongside a running cow, reaching down, and taking it by the tail. A half-wrap was taken on the saddle-horn as the horse went past, and when the cow's hind end came off the ground, it was suddenly released with the same result. A man could throw an animal nearly twice as big as his horse in this fashion quite easily.

Stewart Edward White graphically described this method as practised by the Californios in a series of stories published about sixty years ago in the *Saturday Evening Post*. The series later became the book *The Saga of Andy Burnett*.

(Being totally enthralled with this wonderful story, I was particularly impressed with this trick of throwing a cow, to the point where I wanted to try it. One day when I was helping my father gather the fall cut of beef my chance came. I was working a small bunch of cattle out of the brush. When I came out into the open valley with them, I could see my father holding a bunch in a fence corner on top of a hill on the far side. At that point an old brockle-faced cow that had been giving me plenty of trouble quit the bunch and made a run back toward the brush. I was riding a fine bay horse, my father's top mount, who had undoubtedly forgotten more about cows than I knew, and in a flash he was after her. In about six jumps there was her tail right by my stirrup. Grabbing it, I took a wrap on the saddle-horn and as her hind end swung up in my direction, I turned her tail loose. What happened then was satisfactorily spectacular, for she left the ground in a twisting fall and came down hard right under my horse's nose, whereupon he went over her end over end. I came out of that old slick fork rig like a rock out of a catapult and must have gone twenty feet before I hit the ground. My wind was knocked out so far I was thinking I was never going to get it back. When I finally got my eyes uncrossed and looked back, there we were all strung out about an equal distance apart, my horse and cow in the same shape as me. Properly chastised, the cow stood up first and headed back for the bunch. Then the horse got to his feet, looking as though he didn't know which direction was Sunday. About that time my father arrived to give me a proper chewing out as I was gathering myself up to discover if everything was still working more or less. He opened his salty dissertation by asking, "What the hell are you trying to do? Kill my horse?" For some reason or other, I have never tried that trick again to this day. However, I know it works, even if not as expected sometimes.)

Those early Texas cow hunters had another trick they sometimes used when they caught a large bunch of longhorns in one of their traps. They roped the cattle one by one and sewed their eyes shut. Then they brought some tame oxen, wearing bells on a strap around their necks as usual, and let them mingle with the blinded ones. In this way they could handle them by pushing them into a gathering of other cattle and letting them graze together. When such cattle became accustomed to depending on hearing the bells for keeping contact with other cattle, they could be pushed along with a driven herd and by the time the stitches came loose, they were in unfamiliar range and sufficiently tractable to be trailed to whatever destination was required. It was very inhumane by today's standards, but it worked. It took a special breed of man to handle those Texas longhorns, but handle them they did.

It was here that the North American cattle industry was born, for these men, who knew the meaning of being truly tough, went to work to rebuild shattered dreams and to take advantage of a new market for beef being opened up to the north and east. When a new market showed up in Kansas upon the building of the first railroad that would eventually become a transcontinental route across America, they began putting together herds and trailed them north to Abilene, Dodge, and other towns. It was the beginning of a kind of bovine migration that was awesome in its enterprise, geographical impacts, and cultural development, apart from its colourful and legendary reputation reaching west and north to the Pacific Coast and the Canadian wilderness.

CHAPTER 1

Trailing Herds
North and West

Trailing cattle to market out of Texas was not something that just happened following the Civil War, for it started when gold was found in California in 1849 and Texas cattlemen realized that there was a good market there. Anyone observing a gold rush with all its feverish heterogeneous mixture of people knows that supplying the inevitable demand for provisions, especially food, is where real profits lay.

One Texan by the name of John Hackett, who had ridden west to the California gold fields on the upper reaches of the Sacramento River in 1849, was not overly impressed with the chances of striking a rich claim, but he saw another opportunity to make some money. So he pointed his horse east and rode back to Arkansas to buy some cattle – 937 head of what were probably American oxen – not longhorns. With the help of a crew of riders, some of them no doubt eager to get their fingers on some gold, he drove his herd west across

Texas following the most travelled southern route. No doubt due to the Indian raids, the lack of water, and quite likely starvation, he lost about three quarters of his cattle, and finally arrived in California with only 182 survivors, but he still made a profit. The miners were hungry for beef and were willing and able to pay for it.

The trail drivers who subsequently headed west from Texas to this market had a choice of routes; there was the smoother southern route that was easy going but short of grass and water and plagued with fierce Apaches and Comanches; or there was a choice of more mountainous routes farther north. One was the trail blazed by John Fremont in 1844 that followed the present Wyoming border west to Salt Lake, and then went southwest across what is now Utah and Nevada to the Mohave River in California. The drivers could also swing west from Salt Lake across northern Nevada to the Humbolt River trail. There was more grass and water on the northern trails, but they were very rough with some high passes, and it is likely most of the cattle went by the southern route.

These trail drives had crews that included some experienced drovers, or cowboys as they were later called, along with some old mountain men, but a good part of the crews were young inexperienced types willing to work their way for the use of a horse or a mule and food. The Apaches were hostile and every man was supplied with a rifle and two Colt revolvers, as well as plenty of ammunition, to fight off Indians. If these Texas cattlemen found the market in California too low, they quickly learned to hold and fatten their cattle on the rich grass till a suitable price allowed them a good profit. What impressions the Californios made on the Texans with their ways of handling cattle is not reported in any great detail. The young *caballeros* from the big ranches there were resplendent in silver-mounted equipment, which probably generated scoffing among the Texans as being use-less "foofaraw," but they may have learned some new rope throws from them and the *vaqueros*. A few of them were very attracted by the lovely *senoritas*, married them, and adopted California as their new home.

The demand for beef had proved to be a bonanza for the Californians, who had many thousands of cattle on their big holdings, and they not only sold their mature steers, but bulls, cows, and young stock as well. While the enterprising Texans had it very good for a while and trailed many herds of cattle over onto the Pacific slope, by 1856 the market was glutted to the point where there was no profit for them. By 1859 the cattle coming from Texas had slowed to a mere trickle. It was then the Texans began dreaming of driving their cattle north toward the Missouri River to take advan-tage of approaching railroads and eastern markets.

The first cattle drive north from Texas was made by a man named Thomas Candy Ponting, who was born in England and had experience driving cattle to market there. He came to Illinois at age sixteen, worked with cattle, and then went into the business of buying stock and trailing them to Wisconsin to sell to the new settlers. When he was twenty-three years old, he and his partner, Washington Malone, heard about cheap cattle in Texas, so they headed south by saddlehorse and wagon, until they finally arrived in the coun-try just south of the Red River. They bought 780 longhorns and hired a crew of Texans to help drive them north.

To just tell of such an enterprise can be very prosaic unless one looks carefully at a map of the United States and lets one's imagination picture what it was like to venture forth from Illinois with horses and a wagon to find a way through wild country for about a thousand miles as the crow flies, and for quite a bit more if one could calculate the winding of the trail. Some of the journey would follow established roads and trails, but much of it would be through virgin country where only Indian trails were present, if any. The drive would have to detour around heavy growths of forest, where the wagon could not go without much axe-work. In this day where enterprise is enhanced by modern means of travel and communications, it is difficult to realize what it was like to set forth on such an expedition, where the participants had to depend on their ingenuity and determination, with only sketchy information available from occasional people – Indians and white men – encountered along the way. When they got their herd gathered and pointed north with a crew of Texans they had the advantage of backtrailing, but cows being what they are in general and longhorns being a type unto themselves – wild, fleet of foot, and very near as independent as the deer of the country – the task of driving them all the way back to Illinois was something to boggle the mind.

But Ponting and Malone were far from being ordinary men; they were the kind whose eyes gleamed at a challenge, the sort that saw clearly what every step of the trail ahead required. They planned and, when the plans went awry, they improvised, and never stopped moving for very long. Being as keen-minded and physically fit as men can get through interminable hours of living in the saddle, they worked well together.

When they got their cattle gathered, they acquired a big, amiable ox with a bell hanging from a strap around his neck, and tied him to the rear axle of their wagon to act as a lead steer for the herd. And thus the cattle began moving north, fording rivers and weathering storms when they encountered them.

When they got to the Mississippi River, they loaded the cattle on barges and crossed to the other side. Two years from the time they left, they were back in Illinois, where they wintered the herd on corn sheaves. They sold most of the cattle there come spring, but kept 150 of the biggest and best steers, which they planned to sell in New York City. Ponting had heard that he could load the cattle onto railroad cars at Muncie, Indiana, and ship them. But when he got there, he found only boxcars available, which was a disappointment – cattle cars are made with slatted sides which allow cattle to see through them and makes them much easier to load. On top of that there were no holding pens or loading chutes. So they gathered some timber and built a holding pen and a ramp. Loading was rendered a good deal more difficult by the length of the cattle's horns, which were wider than a box-car door, but they managed it and left no record of having trimmed any horns in the process.

In due course, they arrived on the bank of the Hudson River across from New York. No mention was made of the fact that these cattle had been trailed all the way from Texas, and they were sold for a good price, the best of them bringing eighty dollars a head. When the news of their origin got out, the meat was reported in the newspapers as being more like venison than ordinary beef, fine-grained, a little tough, but tasty. It had been a long trail but the longhorns had found a new market. Ponting and Malone were very matter-of-fact about their accomplishment, and made very little mention of the difficulties in their stories of the history-making trek.

Cattle drives were not numerous during the Civil War, but not long afterwards the Texas drovers had the cows back on the move to northern markets along the newly con-structed railroads. After the war, when the Texas men returned to their homesteads, there was a world of longhorns ranging across the land, with estimates of their number running from three to eight million head – many of them unbranded. These "slick" ones were called mavericks and there is a story behind the name, or probably more accurately, a whole procession of legends, all centred around an eccentric gentleman by the name of Samuel Maverick. He was a lawyer and didn't know anything about cattle, and obviously had very little intention of learning. What is probably the real explanation of his unique association with cattle was his acquisition of a herd of 400 head given to him by way of paying off a debt. These cattle were unbranded and he put them in charge of a somewhat lazy and shiftless family who were supposed to brand them but never got around to it, with the result that the herd of steers continued to go unmarked. At a meeting of stockmen in southern Texas each man declared publicly what brand and earmark he was using. After everyone had gone on record but Samuel Maverick, he said that seeing as how everybody else was using a mark, he wouldn't use one at all and would appreciate it if everyone recognized all unbranded cattle as his. As he was known to own only a bunch of steers it was agreed. But of course his cattle were thus put in jeopardy – open game to anyone who could put a brand on them. From then on everybody seeing an animal without a brand said, "There goes one of Mr. Maverick's cattle," and before long any cow not wearing a brand became known as a "maverick." But it was agreed by range law that putting a brand on any animal less than a year old was prohibited. That all started back in the 1850s and by the end of the Civil War, Samuel Maverick's herd was beyond counting; there were probably a million or more unbranded cattle running wild in southern Texas.

Many a cowman got his start by branding mavericks, though he was supposed to own a seed-stock of herding cows to make it legitimate. A good portion of those first herds heading north for Abilene in Kansas were mavericks caught in the brushy breaks of southern Texas. Those herds of generally not more than three thousand head apiece were just the beginning of the movement of cattle out of the Lone Star

State. They were made up of wild cattle accustomed, as were the men who drove them, to staying alive in country where conditions ranged from the sublime to pure hell. It took longhorn steers eight to ten years to achieve full growth, but when they did, they were something to catch the eye. They were long-legged, slab-sided, with narrow hips and hoofs like iron, and a set of horns that went from almost straight to corkscrew that could reach a spread of eight feet, though the average was closer to four. Such animals would weigh from sixteen to seventeen hundred pounds, were fleet as deer, designed to travel, able to go for days without water, and often got up out of the bedground at night to make a run without very much excuse. Sometimes, when well trail-broke, they handled as smooth as silk, going day after day for weeks without any trouble. But then something might happen; something as inconsequential as a tumbleweed blowing up against a sleeping steer on the edge of the herd at night, or a foraging skunk wandering among them, and in a split second every animal came up on its feet and in one jump the herd would be running flat-out.

"Stompedes" the Texans called them, and none but the longhorns in the history of cattle in North America had such a hair-trigger affinity to running. The word came from the Spanish – *estampida* – like a lot of others mixed up in ranching lingo, and it is probably best described by an old-timer's definition. "It's one jump to their feet and another jump to hell," as J. Frank Dobie writes in *The Longhorns*. "Stampede" became the word of common usage. Unlike ordinary cattle, longhorns do not get up hind-end first and pause for a moment on their front knees, as though praying, before coming up on their feet. They make it up in one motion, like deer, sometimes with the whole herd rising as one in the wink of an eye, motivated as if an electrical switch had been flicked.

The worst stampedes occurred at night, sometimes in a stygian darkness broken only by the flashes of lightning during a thunderstorm. The cowmen dreaded not so much the danger of stampedes but the potential loss of cattle. Anyone who has not been out in a storm on a horse, with thunder blasting like artillery and lightning flashing, cannot even come close to imagining what it is like. It is even harder to visualize the wild riding required to turn two or three thousand running cattle, or to imagine the sound of their hoofs blotting out the roaring of the storm.

Contrary to popular belief, largely cultivated by writers of westerns, most of whom never saw a stampede or rode with a herd, guns were almost never used to turn stampeding cattle. Any cowboy who ever tried turning a herd by this method was likely to find himself very promptly without a job.

The trick was to ride up alongside the herd to the leaders and then bend them into a mill. Two well-mounted men could do this, though it always took some wild riding with the ever-present danger of a horse stepping into a hole or going over a cut bank. Then, of course, what happened when cattle running behind caught up could be deadly for a rider. Some trail bosses who really knew cattle would only send one or two men to handle a stampede, because that way it was less likely that the herd would be split up into small bunches that made it much harder to round them up.

Stampeding cattle rarely ran more than three or four miles before they began to slow, and it was then easier to bend the leaders one way or the other into a mill. Because animals, like men, are more often "right-handed," leading with the right feet, it was easier to bend them into a circle to the right, and, if circumstances allowed, the cowboys riding to control a stampede tried to use this tendency in their favour.

The reason trail herds were usually never larger than

three thousand head, give or take a few hundred, was that when a larger herd went into a mill there was the very definite danger that the cattle in the middle of it would go down and be trampled to death. When several herds being driven on the same trail got too close together at a river crossing in a flood or in the vicinity of the destination of shipping pens at a railroad, there was always the danger of a stampeding herd telegraphing their panic to other herds, creating a general mix-up of many thousands of cattle, which could kill hundreds and involve the cowboys in days of hard riding to separate them back into bunches belonging to the different stockmen. This kind of nightmare was always in the minds of owners when trail drives began, and it was a time when the cowboys got little sleep.

In spite of every effort to avoid it, there were times when it happened. There was the occasion in late spring 1882 when the Red River got so high and full of drift logs and clumps of brush floating on the water that it was impossible to cross. Eleven herds, each one accompanied by their cavvy of saddlehorses, were waiting south of the Doan's Crossing one evening when the father of all thunderstorms blew in on the wind. The wind roared, the thunder rumbled like batteries of artillery, the rain came down like waterfalls, hail pounded the earth, and it was as dark as the inside of a cow. A stampede was set off like a match lighting a string of firecrackers. All the herds stampeded, running into each other and milling. In the first streak of dawn not a single outfit had its herd separate; thirty-three thousand cattle were in one grand and terrifying mix, with two thousand or so wild cayuses adding to the confusion, racing back and forth in bunches through the cattle, whinnying for lost companions as they tried to get together and get away. It took one hundred and twenty cowboys ten days to cut out and re-establish their various herds.

Though western writers depict the stampedes as an

enormous danger to cowboys, some of the old trail bosses, who drove many herds of longhorns to market, never knew of one of their cowboys being killed in a stampede, despite their fears. Running cattle would split and thus avoid a dismounted man if there was enough space between them to do so. But if a rider got caught in a mill, it could be a very different story. Cowboy songs told of such happenings, like "When the Work's All Done This Fall," which I myself sang on occasion when I was a boy.

> While riding in the darkness as loudly did he shout,
> Trying his best to head them and turn the herd about,
> His saddlehorse did stumble and on him did fall –
> The poor boy won't see his mother, when the work's
>   all done this fall.

Charles M. Russell, who is without much argument among devotees of western art the finest artist to depict cowboy culture of the era of the longhorn, was also a very good writer, though his books and other publishings were not nearly as numerous as his paintings. Charlie has written what I believe to be quite simply the best and most graphic story ever written of a stampede. Through the voice of his character Rawhide Rawlins, it brings back the colour and flavour of cowboy life as it was lived in that bygone era. Any attempt to retell this wonderful story would be, as Will Rogers put it in the book's introduction, "mighty sad." Here, then, is an excerpt from "Longrope's Last Guard" from *Trails Plowed Under*, first published in 1927.

> "I've read of stampedes that were sure dangerous an' scary, where a herd would run through a camp, upsettin' wagons an' trompin' sleepin' cowpunchers to death. When day broke they'd be fifty or a hundred

miles from where they started, leavin' a trail strewn with blood, dead cowpunchers an' hosses, that looked like the work of a Kansas cyclone. This is all right in books, but the feller that writes 'em is romancin' and don't savvy the cow. Most stampedes is noisy, but harmless to anybody but the cattle. A herd in a bad storm might drift thirty miles in a night, but the worst run I ever see, we ain't four miles from the bed-ground when the day broke.

"This was down in Kansas; we're trailin' beef an' have got about seventeen hundred head. Barrin' a few dry ones the herd's straight steers, mostly Spanish longhorns from down on the Cimarron. We're about fifty miles south of Dodge. Our herd's well broke an' lookin' fine, an' the cowpunchers all good-natured, thinkin' of the good time comin' in Dodge.

"That evenin' when we're ropin' our hosses for night guard, the trail boss, Old Spanish we call him – he ain't no real Spaniard, but he's rode some in Old Mexico an' can talk some Spanish – says to me: 'Them cattle ought to hold well; they ain't been off water four hours, an' we grazed 'em plumb onto the bed-ground. Every hoof of 'em's got a paunch full of grass an' water, an' that's what makes cattle lay good.'

"Me an' a feller named Longrope's on first guard. . . .

"When we reach the bed-ground most of the cattle's already down, lookin' comfortable. They're bedded in open country, an' things look good for an easy night. It's been mighty hot all day, but there's a little breeze now makin' it right pleasant; but down the west I notice some nasty-lookin' clouds hangin' 'round the new moon that's got one horn hooked over the sky-line. The storm's so far off that you can just hear her rumble, but she's walkin' up on us slow, an' I'm hopin' she'll go 'round. The cattle's all layin' quiet an' nice; so me an' Longrope stop to talk awhile.

"'They're layin' quiet,' says I.

"'Too damn quiet,' says he. 'I like cows to lay still all right, but I want some of the natural noises that goes with a herd this size. I want to hear 'em blowin' off, an' the creakin' of their joints, showin' they're easin' themselves in their beds. Listen, an' if you hear anything I'll eat that rimfire saddle of yours – grass rope an' all.'

"I didn't notice till then, but when I straighten my ears it's quiet as a grave. An' if it ain't for the lightnin' showin' the herd once in a while, I couldn't a-believed that seventeen hundred head of longhorns lay within forty feet of where I'm sittin' on my hoss. It's gettin' darker every minute, an' if it wasn't for Longrope's slicker I couldn't a-made him out, though he's so close I could have touched him with my hand. Finally it darkens up so I can't see him at all. It's black as a nigger's pocket; you couldn't find your nose with both hands.'

"I remember askin' Longrope the time.

"'I guess I'll have to get help to find the timepiece,' says he, but gets her feelin' over himself, an', holdin' her under his cigarette takes a long draw, lightin' up her face.

"'Half-past nine,' says he.

"'Half an hour more,' I says. 'Are you goin' to wake up the next guard, or did you leave it to the hoss-wrangler?'

"'There won't be but one guard tonight,' he answers, 'an' we'll ride it. You might as well hunt for a hoss thief in heaven as look for that camp. Well, I guess I'll mosey 'round.' 'An with that he quits me.

"The lightnin's playin' every little while. It ain't makin' much noise, but lights up enough to show where you're at. There ain't no use ridin'; by the flashes I can see that every head's down. For a second it'll be like broad day, then darker than the dungeons of hell, an' I notice the little fire-balls on my hoss's ears; when I spit, there's a streak in the air like strikin' a wet match. These little fire-balls is all I can see of my hoss, an' they tell me he's listenin' all ways; his ears are never still.

"I tell you, there's something mighty ghostly about sittin' up on a hoss you can't see, with them two little blue sparks out in front of you wigglin' an' movin' like a pair of spook-eyes, an' it shows me the old night hoss is usin' his listeners pretty plenty. I got my ears cocked, too, hearing nothin' but Longrope's singin'; he's easy three hundred yards across the herd from me, but I can hear every word:

> *"Sam Bass was born in Injiana,*
> *It was his native home,*
> *'Twas at the age of seventeen*
> *Young Sam began to roam*
> *He first went out to Texas*
> *A cowboy for to be;*
> *A better hearted feller*
> *You'd seldom ever see."*

"It's so plain it sounds like he's singin' in my ear; I can even hear the click-clack of his spur chains against his stirrups when he moves 'round. An' the cricket in his bit – he's usin' one of them hollow conchoed half-breeds – she comes plain to me in the stillness. Once there's a steer layin' on the edge of the herd starts sniffin'. He's takin' long draws of the air, he's nosin' for something. I don't like this, it's a bad sign; it shows he's layin' for trouble, an' all he needs is some little excuse.

"Now every steer, when he beds down, holds his breath for a few seconds, then blows off; that noise is all right an' shows he's settlin' himself for comfort. But when he curls his nose an' makes them long draws it's a sign he's sniffin' for something, an' if anything crosses his wind that he don't like there's liable to be trouble. I've seen dry trail herds mighty thirsty, layin' good till a breeze springs off the water, maybe ten miles away; they start sniffin', an' the minute they get the wind you could comb Texas an' wouldn't have enough punchers to turn 'em till they wet their feet an' fill their paunches.

"I get tired sittin' there starin' at nothin', so start ridin' 'round. Now it's sure dark when animals can't see, but I tell you by the way my hoss moves he's feelin' his way. I don't blame him none; it's like lookin' in a black pot. Sky an' ground all the same, an' I ain't gone twenty-five yards till I hear cattle gettin' up around me; I'm in the herd an' its luck I'm singing an' they don't get scared. Pullin' to the left I work cautious an' easy till I'm clear of the bunch. Ridin's useless, so I flop my weight over on one stirrup an' go on singin'.

"The lightnin's quit now, an' she's darker than ever; the breeze has died down an' it's hotter than the hubs of hell. Above my voice I can hear Longrope. He's singin' the 'Texas Ranger' now; the Ranger's a long song an' there's few punchers that knows it all, but Longrope's sprung a lot of new verses on me an' I'm interested. Seems like he's on about the twenty-fifth verse, an' there's danger of his chokin' down, when there's a whisperin' in the grass behind me; it's a breeze sneakin' up. It flaps the tail of my slicker an' goes by; in another second she hits the herd. The ground shakes, an' they're all runnin'! My hoss takes the scare with 'em an' 's bustin' a hole in the darkness when he throws both front feet in a badger hole, goin' to his knees an' plowin' his nose in the dirt. But he's a good night hoss an' 's hard to keep down. The minute he gets his feet under him he raises, runnin' like a scared wolf. Hearin' the roar behind him he don't care to mix with them locoed longhorns. I got my head turned over my shoulder listenin', tryin' to make out which way they're goin', when there's a flash of lightnin' busts a hole in the sky – it's one of these kind that puts the fear of God in a man, thunder an' all together. My hoss whirls an' stops in his tracks, spraddlin' out an' squattin' like he's hit, an' I can feel his heart beatin' agin my leg, while mine's poundin' my ribs like it'll bust through. We're both plenty scared.

"This flash lights up the whole country, givin' me a glimpse of the herd runnin' a little to my left. Big drops of rain are pounding on my hat. The storm has broke now for sure, with the lightnin' bombardin' us at every jump. Once a flash shows me Longrope, ghostly in his wet slicker. He's so close to me that I could hit him with my quirt an' I hollers to him, 'This is hell.'

"'Yes,' he yells back above the roar, 'I wonder what damned fool kicked the lid off.'

"I can tell by the noise that they're runnin' straight; there ain't no clickin' of horns. It's a kind of hummin' noise like a buzz-saw, only a thousand times louder. There's no use in tryin' to turn 'em in this darkness, so

I'm ridin' wide – just herdin' by ear an' follerin' the noise. Pretty soon my ears tell me they're crowdin' an' comin' together; the next flash shows 'em all millin', with heads jammed together an' horns locked; some's rared up ridin' others, an' these is squirmin' like bristled snakes. In the same light I see Longrope, an' from the blink I get of him he's among 'em or too close for safety, an' in the dark I thought I saw a gun flash three times with no report. But with the noise these longhorns are makin' now, I doubt if I could a-heard a six-gun bark if I pulled the trigger myself, an' the next thing I know me an' my hoss go over a bank, lightin' safe. I guess it ain't over four feet, but it seems like fifty in the darkness, an' if it hadn't been for my chin string I'd a-went from under my hat. Again the light shows me we're in a 'royo with the cattle comin' over the edge, wigglin' an' squirmin' like army worms.

"It's a case of all night riding. Sometimes they'll mill an' quiet down, then start trottin' an' break into a run. Not till daybreak do they stop, an' maybe you think old day ain't welcome. My hoss is sure leg-weary, an' I ain't so rollicky myself. When she gets light enough, I begin lookin' for Longrope, with nary a sign of him; an' the herd, you wouldn't know they were the same cattle – smeared with mud an' ga'nt as greyhounds; some of 'em with their tongues still lollin' out from their night's run. But sizin' up the bunch, I guess I got 'em all. I'm kind of worried about Longrope. It's a cinch that wherever he is he's afoot, an' chances is he's layin' on the prairie with a broken leg.

"The cattle's spread out, an' they begin feedin'. There ain't much chance of losin' 'em, now it's broad daylight, so I ride up on a rise to take a look at the back trail. While I'm up there viewin' the country, my eyes run onto somethin' a mile back in a draw. I can't make it out, but get curious, so spurrin' my tired hoss into a lope I take the back trail. 'Taint no trouble to foller in the mud; it's plain as plowed ground. I ain't rode three hundred yards till the country raises a little an' shows me this thing's a hoss, an' by the white streak on his flank I heap savvy it's Peon – that's the hoss Longrope's ridin'. When I get close he whinners pitiful like; he's lookin' for sympathy, an' I notice, when he turns to face me, his right foreleg's broke. He's sure a sorry sight with that fancy, full-stamped, center-fire saddle hangin' under his belly in the mud. While I'm lookin' him over, my hoss cocks his ears to the right, snortin' low. This scares me – I'm afeared to look. Somethin' tells me I won't see Longrope, only part of him – that part that stays here on earth when the man's gone. Bracin' up, I foller my hoss's ears, an' there in the holler of the 'royo is a patch of yeller; it's part of a slicker. I spur up to get a better look over the bank, an' there tromped in the mud is all there is left of Longrope. Pullin' my gun I empty her in the air. This brings the boys that are follerin' on the trail from the bed-ground. Nobody'd to tell 'em we'd had hell, so they come in full force, every man but the cook an' hoss-wrangler.

"Nobody feels like talkin'. It don't matter how rough men are – I've known 'em that never spoke without cussin', that claimed to fear neither God, man, nor devil – but let death visit camp an' it puts 'em thinkin'. They generally take their hats off to this old boy that comes everywhere an' any time. He's always ready to pilot you – willin' or not – over the long dark trail that folks don't care to travel. He's never welcome, but you've got to respect him.

"'It's tough – damned tough,' says Spanish, raisin' poor Longrope's head an' wipin' the mud from his face with his neck-handkerchief, tender, like he's feared he'll hurt him. We find his hat tromped in the mud not far from where he's layin'. His scabbard's empty, an' we never do locate his gun.

"That afternoon when we're countin' out the herd to see if we're short any, we find a steer with a broken shoulder an' another with a hole plumb through his nose. Both these is gun wounds; this accounts for them flashes I see in the night. It looks like, when Longrope gets mixed in the mill, he tries to gun his way out, but the cattle crowd him to the bank an' he goes over. The chances are he was dragged from his hoss in a tangle of horns.

"Some's for takin' him to Dodge an' gettin' a box made for him, but Old Spanish says: 'Boys, Longrope is a prairie man, an' if she was a little rough at times, she's been a good foster mother. She cared for him while he's awake, let her nurse him in his sleep.' So we wrapped him in his blankets, an' put him to bed.

"It's been twenty years or more since we tucked him in with the end-gate of the bed-wagon for a headstone, which the cattle have long since rubbed down, leavin' the spot unmarked. It sounds lonesome, but he ain't alone, 'cause these old prairies has cradled many of his kind in their long sleep."

These men who trailed the longhorns north in ever-increasing thousands were every bit as unique as the animals with which they worked. They shared a certain affinity for nature in their common origins, in ways of life developed through their exposure to the wilds, from the brush-choked breaks along the Rio Grande, to the great oceans of grass waving in the wind, under the vast dome of the sky to the north and west in a glory of space and freedom. The cowboys exercised their wills in a determination to move the longhorns from their home ranges to new and unfamiliar territory in spite of hostile Indians, the pure hell of earth-shaking storms at night, flooded rivers, and great distances; and the cayuses they rode were the catalyst that made it possible.

The cowboys were skilful in their work with the longhorns, exercising a certain psychological knowledge to head them in the right direction and keep them going slow enough to allow them to gain weight, or at least hold it on a level, allowing maximum profit at the end of the trail, but fast enough to get there before their own supplies ran out. They not only knew cattle and horses but could think like them and often anticipated what they would do in a given situation in time to control them and avoid trouble. But real trouble could not always be averted by their skills, in the dark of night on the bedgrounds, when the sharp forks of lightning flashed and struck the ground to the accompaniment of the drums of thunder. Then cowboy culture was on the move.

From the very beginning of man's association with the horse, his social status has been elevated the minute he stepped up in the saddle. He not only became a more efficient hunter but also a much more effective warrior. At a time when nearly all of North America was either on horseback or on wheels being pulled by horses, the Texas cowboy was not unique in using a horse, but he was distinguishing himself by the way he used it for his work with longhorns. And as men on horseback had done since the first horse was broken to ride, his dress and equipment took on characteristics synonymous with his occupation, putting him in a peerless stratum in equestrian society – there was nothing quite like him anywhere in the world. From his wide-brimmed hat to his spurs and boots, he was different, and every item of his equipment – saddle, bridle, lariat, quirt, and guns – was designed to fit his kind of work.

Courageous and as physically tough as men can get, he was inordinately loyal to the brand he worked for and his capacity for endurance was monumental. Generally soft-spoken, he could be colourful and sometimes dismally profane, but shy to the point of being almost mute in the presence of a decent woman, and very gentle in her company. Yet when the opportunity arose, he would seek out a lady for the evening to enjoy a frolic in her bed with utter abandon. He might be good, bad, or indifferent in his approach to law and order or what was generally recognized as morality; yet his friends could count on him to stand with them in a tight spot. If he failed on this, he had better have a good reason, for second chances were very rare.

Because of the very nature of his work, where danger was a fact of life, and because he never knew at what instant it would strike, he was always armed or within easy reach of a gun. When he got up in the morning, the first thing he put on was his hat and the last his gunbelt with its cartridge loops and holstered six-shooter. Often used for signalling, the gun was essential to stop a charging cow bent on killing his horse and him when, in the middle of a wreck, his mount might be down and his leg trapped under it. It could be very handy to punctuate the positive when, say, somebody claimed a cow belonging to his outfit, or when he needed to protect the trail herd from raiding Indians. Some cowboys went all their lives without ever pulling a gun in anger, yet let some idiot, per-haps made brave by too much drink, threaten him or one of his crew in a saloon at the end of a drive and drawing a gun was second nature and the use of it very deadly, for the range was usually short. The man who killed in self-defence gener-ally went scot-free by unwritten frontier law. The victim acquired a small piece of real-estate of indeterminate title in a graveyard where headstones were scarce and even head-boards might be overlooked.

Contrary to the popular belief generated first by western writers city-born and -raised, and later by Hollywood, very few cowboys ever carried more than one pistol for the simple reason that a gun and its necessary accoutrements were heavy. None with any sense ever carried more than five cartridges in a six-shooter, because if he dropped the gun it had the nasty habit of falling on its hammer, which generally sheared off the half-cock safety notch and allowed it to fire.

One bronc-buster tells of riding a horse whose bucking sent his gun flying out of its holster to the ground, where it went off. He retrieved the gun and it wasn't till later he discovered a .45-calibre hole in the brim of his hat, where a bullet had passed within an inch of his head. That cowboy thereafter became a devotee of loading only five shots in his six-shooter.

The classic and dramatic picture of two individuals going into a duelling strut, to meet in the middle of a dusty street at high noon, to draw with lightning speed and shoot it out, is for the large part a myth. It makes for romance, but it was not in the pattern. If there was time, the cowboy walking into danger went with gun in hand ready to use. But there were exceptions. James Butler (Wild Bill) Hickok was likely the most deadly gunfighter the West ever saw. He could get his guns into action in a flash and was an unerring shot with either hand – a very rare skill indeed. He was not a cowboy, but a professional gambler, and the marshal of Abilene for a while. He has been credited with killing seventy-three men in his lifetime, and they didn't count Indians in those days. He was murdered in the Black Hills by Jack McCall, who sneaked up and shot him from behind.

Other famous gunfighters were Bat Masterson and Wyatt

Earp. Bat Masterson was a marshal and a very brave man. But he died from wounds suffered in a gunfight. Wyatt Earp was also a lawman, who preferred to avoid killing by batting uncooperative lawbreakers over the head with his pistol barrel and then dragging them off to jail. He was known to have taken on five men at once and knocked them all out in this fashion. He had a long career as a marshal and lived to be well up in his eighties before dying peacefully in California.

Then there was Wallace Reid, the well-known Montana marshal, well-liked, cool, and efficient, besides being highly respected as a superlative pistol shot and rifleman. His reputation was such that on one occasion a horse thief he was pursuing on the open prairie recognized his pursuer, unbuckled his gunbelt, and threw it down beside the trail before pulling his horse to a stop and surrendering. He wanted it plainly evident that he was unarmed. When Wallace Reid died of a ruptured appendix some years later, his brother Jack fell heir to that gun and I had the opportunity to examine it. The holster and cartridge belt were made of light saddle leather lined with calfskin, and both were beautifully tooled with a fine basket design. The gun was a .44-40 Colt six-shooter in good condition, though well-worn. The former owner obviously took care of his equipment and knew how to use it, but was plainly just as aware of his limitations and was no fast-draw artist – the holster was too deep. The fast draw so widely featured in western stories and motion pictures was not possible with the average holster then in use, which was made to carry the gun, not for speed in getting it into action. The gun was worn fairly high on the hip so as not to interfere with a rider's movement. Some holsters were shorter, and these had a thong with a fixed loop attached on the holster at the top; the loop was slipped over the hammer-spur of the gun to prevent it from being shaken loose on a bucking horse or from whatever other rough jolting might occur. This loop could be readily released by the rider's thumb, allowing the pistol to be drawn. To most of those old-time cowboys working with longhorn cattle, the six-shooter was a weapon to be used when necessary in defence and played with in moments of exuberance, but pointing it away from themselves was as natural as breathing.

When they finally arrived at a town at the end of a long trail drive, the cowboys were sometimes moved to celebrate by riding at full speed along the main street, firing their pistols in the air or into the ground while yelling like Indians on the warpath. It was generally harmless enough fun, but townspeople not surprisingly frowned on it, so they hired a marshal to keep the peace. Such a lawman, if he was the right type and sufficiently courageous and experienced enough to lay down the law and enforce it, could tame a town to a point of quietness. A rule was imposed that all pistols be hung up at a designated place and left there while the owners were in town. This could render some element of peaceful atmosphere if applied properly and undoubtedly could save some lives, when whiskey touched off a quarrel; but it required a marshal with the kind of reputation to make it stick with the Texans, a type not always available. The cowtowns along the railroad were very rough places, a long call from what the quiet easterners, who ran most of the businesses, were accustomed to living with.

The cowboys rode half-wild horses, worked with wild cattle, and were themselves far from tame. It was the cattle and the need for markets for them that set the whole expanse of the plains into motion, and there were no cows in the history of the species better adapted for migration than the longhorns. Their drives to the north were not exactly tours of pleasure, for they ran into much trouble with Indians, who demanded more than just a steer or two for meat, but insisted that they stay on a designated trail, and also that every herd pay a head fee for cattle crossing Indian lands. This tax generally amounted to about ten cents per cow and very few of the drovers refused to pay it.

The longhorns were infected with ticks, which were carriers of Texas fever, a cattle disease to which the longhorns were immune but which was deadly to northern cattle. Consequently, passage to longhorn herds was often refused in Kansas and other states. So-called Jayhawkers, who were nothing but extortionists preying on the herds, gave the Texas trail drivers a bad time. Baxter Springs was a hellhole with its population of outlaws and blockaders, and its red-light district, saloons, and gambling houses. It was the destination of many of the herds in the late 1860s but the Jayhawkers there made life so miserable for the Texans that they abandoned it for such places as Abilene, Ellesworth, Newton, Wichita, and Dodge City to the west, which progressively became equally lively capitals of sin and corruption.

One driver by the name of Story, who took a herd to Baxter Springs and found the place clotted with blockaded herds, decided to do something about it. He had been west and taken part in the gold rush at Virginia City, where he had accumulated some gold with which he had purchased his cattle. So he swung the herd west to Fort Leavenworth. There he bought a string of wagons and loaded them with provisions, hitched up teams of oxen to them, and hired bullwhackers to drive them. With this caravan and his steers he took the Oregon Trail and eventually crawled up the valley of the Platte River to Fort Laramie, Wyoming. There the army officers in command forbade him to go any farther because the Sioux were on the warpath.

The officers also ordered him to camp several miles out from the fort so that his stock would not eat the grass needed by the cavalry horses. He was so far from the fort that he was at the mercy of an Indian attack, so he outfitted his twenty-seven cowboys with new Remington breechloading rifles, and plenty of ammunition, and headed out. The attack that the army had predicted was not long coming, for some Sioux hit them not far from Fort Reno, wounding two cowboys with their arrows, and then swept away with part of the herd. Story immediately pursued them into the hills, surprised the Indians in camp, and took the cattle away from them. He left his wounded men at the fort and proceeded on to Fort Phil Kearny, which was under the command of Colonel Carrington. The colonel flatly ordered Story to stay at Fort Phil Kearny, but again so far from the post that it could offer no protection. It was an impossible situation and Story knew he was damned if he did and damned if he didn't obey orders. So he called the crew together and took a vote. Only one man voted against moving out, whereupon Story pointed his six-shooter at him and took him prisoner so that he could not inform the soldiers. That night they drove the whole outfit around the fort and disappeared into the Indian country. When they were a day out, Story released his prisoner and said he could go back, but the man was afraid to go alone and chose to remain with the crew. They moved the cattle and wagons at night and grazed them during the day.

Twice the Sioux attacked the crawling procession, and they killed one man out hunting meat for the party. There were about three thousand Indian warriors in the country and only twenty-odd cowboys, but they were deadly with their Remington rifles and they stood the Indians off.

They had left Fort Phil Kearny on October 22. On December 9, 1866, the entire herd and wagon train-load of groceries rolled into Virginia City, where Story's young wife, whom he had left there, greeted him warmly. He had not lost one steer anywhere along that long trail. The Sioux were very angry and they closed the trail behind him. It was four years before another trail drive used it.

Another trailblazer was Charles Goodnight, who had been a freighter driving bull teams before the war. During the war he had served four years with the Texas Rangers. After the war he went into the cow business. When other Texans were driving north, he looked west, knowing there was a market there in New Mexico. The Indians had been subdued and were on a reservation near Fort Summer. The U.S. Government had to buy rations for these Indians, as well as for the soldiers, and needed beef. Goodnight knew that the best way there was the shortest, but also the driest, for to try to swing a herd north was dangerous, as numerous Comanches were on the warpath.

Fortunately he ran into Oliver Loving, who was likely the most experienced trail driver in Texas, and outlined to him his plan to drive a herd across the Staked Plains, a dry stretch of desert where there was one waterless piece of country over ninety miles across from the Middle Concho to Horsehead Crossing on the Pecos River. At first Loving warned him about the dangers involved in this proposed route, but the sheer boldness of the idea took hold of him and he asked to join Goodnight on the drive. So they gathered a mixed herd of twenty-five hundred head, which proved to be a mistake, for some of the cows had calves at heel and they were unable to keep up. Shooting the calves came hard and Goodnight swore never to drive a mixed herd again on this Horsehead trail.

When the dreaded dry stretch began, the herd walked with bitter alkali dust lifting in clouds and the men rode masked with their neckerchiefs pulled up over their noses. That night the cattle never bedded down, but just milled and moaned while the whole crew worked to hold them.

The second day the herd kept on. They had a big chuck-wagon, drawn by six pairs of oxen, carrying barrels that provided some water for the crew and horses. That night, knowing it was useless to try to hold the herd, they walked the animals all night. By the third day, the water was gone, and the stock and men were nearly crazed with thirst. Thirst was a tangible and terrible condition which men and animals just endured. Now they had to keep the cattle going, for if any lay down, they would never get up. They had a bell on one of the lead rider's horses so that the drag riders could hear it. When it could no longer be heard, a cowboy was sent ahead to hold the leaders till the drag caught up.

On the fourth morning they dropped down through Castle Gap and were greeted by a cool breeze, and the cattle nearly stampeded as they imagined that they smelled water. As they came out of the gap, they could see the Pecos River twelve miles away. The cattle were so wild with thirst that when they came to the river they plunged in, swam across, and turned around to swim back before they drank.

If anything proved the amazing ability of longhorns to handle tough going, this was it. Goodnight and Loving lost only three hundred cattle in spite of their mixed herd of steers, cows, and young animals. After resting and grazing the cattle along the Pecos, they drove them north to Fort Sumner, where the Indians rejoiced, for they were nearly starving. There they sold their beef steers for eight cents a pound live weight, an unheard-of price.

Loving took the remainder of the herd – stock cows and bulls – on north to Colorado, while Goodnight hastened back to Texas to gather another herd. On the way Loving crossed Raton Pass, where a tough, irascible old mountain man had built a trail. His name was Uncle Dick Hooten and he demanded and got a toll of ten cents a head for use of his trail, which made Loving angry. But when Loving arrived in

Denver, he sold the herd for a good price and that helped his feelings some.

Meanwhile, Goodnight gathered a herd of top steers, all mature, rugged animals, and on that trip he lost only five head. But he had to hold them in New Mexico when winter caught up to him there.

The partners had established a great cattle trail and opened up a new trend for the marketing of Texas longhorns. The part from Fort Summer to Denver was known as the Goodnight-Loving Trail. It was every bit as great an endeavour as Story's trip to Virginia City.

Selling cattle was important, but the acquisition of new range was just as attractive to the cattlemen moving cattle north and west. The Sioux were holding the great grazing country of Wyoming, Montana, and the Dakotas, and were fiercely determined not to lose it. In the meantime the hide hunters had been busy exterminating the southern buffalo herds, but there were still millions in the northern herds.

At Fort Phil Kearny, Red Cloud's warriors had been steadily harassing the soldiers. Captain Fetterman's command had been totally wiped out, and Colonel Carrington was understandably very nervous and what boiled down to outright timorous about further mix-ups with the Sioux. The Indian raiders were so persistent that Fort Phil Kearny had trouble keeping enough firewood on hand. Woodcutting details went out under cavalry escort and on one historic occasion gave the Sioux a lesson.

Bill Reid, a real salty frontiersman, had a woodcutting contract at the fort and took his wagons up into the mountains to load them. The teamsters were all armed with new Henry .44 rimfire rifles that held sixteen cartridges in their magazines. They also wore two Colt revolvers that used the same ammunition, and every wagon had a case of 500 rounds. These teamsters were far better armed than the small troop of cavalry guarding them, who used the government-issue single-shot Springfield breechloaders in .45-70 calibre, which had the nasty habit of jamming when fired fast. The wood detail was coming down a long slope when Red Cloud and a big bunch of warriors jumped them.

Bill Reid saw them coming in time to wheel his wagons into a circle on a flat bench, where the wagons were upset with the wheels out — what amounted to an instant fort. With the horses inside the circle, the cavalrymen and teamsters met Red Cloud's charge with a withering fire. Although the records don't always agree, there were thirty-two men defending the wagons and perhaps a thousand Sioux attacking them. Red Cloud just couldn't believe so few could whip him, but all of the teamsters were sharpshooters and the cavalry did its part. The Indians tried again and again, losing warriors every time. Finally the Indians quit and disappeared. Had it not been for Bill Reid's teamsters and their deadly guns, it would have been a very different story. But army reports do not even mention them. My friend Jack Reid, his youngest son, told me this story. Bill Reid was chief of scouts under Colonel George Crook when his cavalry took a beating from the Sioux at the battle of Rosebud Creek in Montana on June 17, 1876. Just nine days later General George Armstrong Custer brashly attacked the biggest gathering of Sioux that was ever brought together, under Sitting Bull, Crazy Horse, Gall, and Little Wolf, in the famous Battle of the Little Bighorn. Custer's cavalry was wiped out to the last man.

But the sun was setting for the warlike Sioux. Not only were their buffalo rapidly disappearing, but the U.S. military launched a heavy campaign which drove Sitting Bull into Canada and ultimately reduced the rest of the Sioux bands onto reservations. This opened up an ocean of grass to the Texas herds that were coming north in what amounted to a bovine flood. The buffalo virtually disappeared from that country in one year. North and South Dakota were soon taken up by ranchers. The great sweep of grass in Montana, suddenly emptied of buffalo in 1882-83, was filled with long-horns within two years.

F. Glidden, who lived in DeKalb, Illinois, in 1874, found himself in an argument with his cattle, which persisted in breaking through a smooth wire fence around his pasture. In repairing it, he noticed hanging from the wire some sharp pointed staples that were used to fasten it to the posts and he had an inspiration. He began to experiment with various methods of fastening barbs to his wire. On November 24, 1874, he took out a patent on his invention, whereupon he set up a factory to manufacture what was then known as Glidden wire. Barbed wire, as it soon became known, was launched on the market, and it was not long before big ranches in Texas began to see its advantages. It did more to tame the west than all the Colt six-shooters and Winchester rifles ever did. But on occasions when ranchers discovered waterholes had been claimed and fenced off, quarrels flared up and sometimes guns came into play.

There were great grass-covered tracts of land throughout the west that carried no cattle for the simple reason that there was no water. But there were huge aquiferous beds – great sheets of water lying underground not far from the surface – which could be tapped by digging wells. At first some primitive windmills were installed at great expense on the Texas panhandle. These were gradually improved and then quicker methods of drilling wells and casing them with iron pipes sped up access to the underground water. The big ranches hired men to do nothing else but service and maintain windmills pumping water into tanks where cattle could drink.

The cattle drives heading north and west toward the open grasslands of Wyoming and Montana now found themselves trailing their herds in dusty lanes fenced off by barbed wire protecting various crops. The horizon was broken every- where by windmill towers.

Although the great cattle drives from Texas were now at a mere trickle, there was still a huge stretch of open-range country extending north from the international boundary to the bush country in Canada – an area that was then desig- nated as the North-West Territories.

CHAPTER 2

Saddles and the
Men Who Rode Them

DON BRESTLER 93.

By the time the Americans came to Texas, the Mexicans had been making saddles for three hundred and fifty years. At that time American saddles had no pommels for wrapping or tying a rope around, so it wasn't long before the Texans adapted the Mexican style. The early Mexican saddles had had no pommel either, so the Mexican *vaqueros* either tied their ropes to the rigging ring that held the cinch, or to the horse's tail, which was not very satisfactory, because the sudden jerk of a roped animal could break the saddle off the horse or even pull off the horse's tail. So the *vaqueros* began making a more suitable saddle by carving the tree (the wooden frame that fit the horse's back) out of wood with a flat-topped horn in front for wrapping or tying their *reatas* (more on these later). The rigging with the metal rings to which the cinch was fastened was made of heavy leather straps fitted over the tree; a cantle sloped up from the rear of

the tree to make the seat. The stirrup leathers hung down on each side to hold the stirrups, which were carved out of solid oak and made to accommodate bare feet, for most *vaqueros* could not afford boots. These first saddles were very simple and bare of any kind of skirt, but the Mexicans lined them with sheepskin to go against the horse's back and sometimes fastened another piece across the seat for some comfort to the rider.

In the beginning the *vaqueros* used an iron-tipped lance, similar to the kind used in Spain, to work the cattle. The lances were used to separate the cows to check their brands and as a prod to move and direct them. In the 1500s, when cattle had increased in New Spain by countless thousands and were so numerous that hides were much more valuable than meat, the lance gave way to the *desjarretadera*, or what is known as a hocking knife. It had a sharp concave blade, about a foot long, fastened crosswise on the end of a stout pole about ten or twelve feet long. A mounted *vaquero* steadied the shaft under his arm with the knife held forward and chased the cow he wanted. As he neared the animal he held the blade so the right hind leg would strike the sharp edge, which cut the tendon. When the tendon on the other leg was cut the animal lay helpless on the ground. Then the *vaquero* dismounted and dispatched the cow with a hard thrust of the knife into its neck just back of the horns, thereby severing the spinal cord. He would remove the hide and peg it flat to the ground to dry. It was a gruesome process, but there were no slaughterhouses in those days and the killing of cattle was done in the open. This was the process used to harvest cowhides by the thousands on various ranches, but naturally if some animals belonging to other ranches were killed, it was too late to do much about it.

So the braided rawhide *reata* came into use. *Reatas* were generally plaited from four strands of rawhide that had been cut evenly from untanned side leather that had had the hair removed. At first the *vaqueros'* method was to hang one end of the *reata* from a pole in a noose and place it over the head of the cow or bull, tying the other end of the *reata* to the horse's tail or the saddle rigging, as has been mentioned. But at best this was an awkward method. If the pole or the loop was dropped, it had to be retrieved, and by that time the animal was likely long-gone. So the *vaqueros* learned to throw the loop and it was then that the *reata* or the *lazo* became a very efficient tool. And when the *vaqueros* began using different throws to fit the circumstances of the moment, the art of the *reata* became even more refined.

A rawhide rope was too often broken when tied solid around a pommel, for when a horse and a bull or a cow tightened it with a sudden jerk the strain was terrific. So the *vaqueros* learned to dally the rope, wrapping it around the horn so that the rope could be allowed to slide a bit when a heavy animal hit the end of it. The *vaquero* could then play his catch like a fish on a line, giving and taking a bit to ease the strain. A good *reata* was braided with the strands running full length with no splices. The *vaqueros* preferred to use the hide from animals of solid colour, for they had learned that skins of spotted animals were weaker at the junction of different coloured spots. The best hides for cutting the rawhide strings came from mature animals. The art of braiding was likely brought over from Spain by the priests who taught it to the young *vaqueros*.

While four strands were generally used for making ropes, six or eight, and sometimes up to thirty-two strands, were eventually employed in the plaiting of bridles, reins, quirts, and hackamores of truly artistic design. Rawhide was wetted, stretched, allowed to dry, then wetted again, before it was braided. During the braiding the strings were kept wet in a vessel of water, with one end of the strands tied together around the limb of a tree or on an iron hook on the ceiling of a building, and as each strand was laid it was given a strong pull by the braider, the pull being kept even every time. The strands were kept flat with no twists so that the finished article was smooth. When a rope was completed, it was thoroughly soaked and stretched again, then allowed to dry. Finally, melted tallow was worked into it by hand to make it waterproof and pliable. Generally a new rope was dragged behind a horse to break it in so that it was evenly flexible throughout its length. Such ropes were generally sixty to seventy feet long and a skilful roper could use all of it in throwing a loop. But some made their ropes longer. There are records of ropes up to one hundred and ten feet long.

The Mexicans also developed the use of maguey root fibre to manufacture twisted ropes that were also used for making *reatas*. The maguey plant grows on semi-desert hills and mountain slopes, which, over a period of five to six years to reach maturity, develops a huge egg-shaped bulbous root two feet or more in diameter. The pulp of this root is used to make the very potent drink tequila, as well as a kind of beer known as pulque. The long fibres of the root are a by-product from which is made the smooth, hard-twist maguey rope. Lariats made from this rope become as stiff as wire when wet and as soft as a dishrag when dried out. If kept dry, this rope is very lively, throws fast, and holds a loop very well. But it will break when it's tied hard and fast, so is good only for light work, and was popular only in a country with a dry climate.

The Texans preferred rawhide ropes at first and later used lariats made from long-strand hemp grown in the Philippines. The hemp was manufactured by the Plymouth Cordage Company, of Plymouth, Massachusetts, and was designated as yacht-line. My father used this rope, which was seven-sixteenths of an inch in diameter, all his active life. It was smooth three-strand hard-twist with a rolled strip of paper in the middle of each strand bearing the company's name about every six inches. I learned to rope with Plymouth yacht-line and used it for years before nylon rope was developed.

In the beginning there were no saddlemakers so the *vaqueros* made their own, but as time went on saddlemaking became something of an art practised by people supplying the demand. There were also specialists in braiding with rawhide and others who tanned leather.

Tanning leather was a slow process. Hides with the hair removed were placed in vats located out in the open, preferably in a shady spot, in which water (generally rainwater) and oak bark were blended to make the tanning fluid. At regular intervals the hides were shifted and turned over so they received equal exposure to the liquid. After nine or ten months they were taken out and dried. The result was fine leather that was both strong and pliable. Later in California this process was improved by the addition of fir bark to the mixture, which gave the leather a permanent deep russet colour. The saddlemakers using bark called their leather "hand-laid oak-tanned saddle skirting," and there is still no better leather found in the world. A few tanneries still make it by the old process.

My present personal saddle, made to order for me forty years ago by N. Porter Company, saddlemakers in Phoenix, Arizona, is made with this leather. It is a bit worn here and there, the fenders and stirrup leathers are getting thin, but the full flower tooling is very attractive on this handsome old saddle that has been ridden many thousands of miles in all kinds of weather over the roughest country – the Canadian Rockies and foothills. Of course, it has been kept clean and oiled as well as repaired over the years.

North American saddlemakers all had their own ideas of comfort, durability, and practicality in building their saddles, but they also built many saddles to special order for cowboys who had their own positive ideas of what their personal rigging should be. These saddles ran from no-frills plain leather, some with the rough side out, to those stamped in a basket pattern, and to some that were works of art in full flower hand tooling. Wally McRae expressed his modest thoughts on his old rough-side-out saddle in a poem:

I'll never get all of that fancy tack
Even if I could
Cause you better be as good as you look
And I just ain't that good.

There were other fancy-Dan cowboys, who dressed in the best clothes money could buy, from their 10x beaver hats to their skintight silk-stitched and inlaid boots with silver-mounted engraved spurs, and rigging to match, including tooled or fancy-braided bridles, silver-mounted bits, full flower tooled saddles with pockets adorned with long bear-skin or sealskin lids and matching twenty-four-inch tooled *tapaderos*, plus some sterling silver trim all around. These boys were the fashion models of the plains and were some-times viewed with suspicion by ranch foremen when they rode in looking for work. You could see the sun flash off these riders long before they were close enough to recognize. One thing you could be sure of: they were either very stupid or very honest, for no cowboy looking over his shoulder because of a bad conscience or fear of being found would dare ride with all that silver reflecting the sun. It was likely most of them never rode much in brush country, for gather-ing wild cows in the scrub timber was no place for such things as fancy rigging with silver inlays. But some of these fancy

Dans could ride anything with hair on it, and knew what a cow said to her calf.

I remember running into one heading up the Oldman River in the Alberta Rockies about fifty years ago while I was guiding a hunting party with my pack outfit. He was a tall, good-looking young man, the picture of sartorial elegance in his bearskin chaps as he sat his saddle, a beautiful Visalia slick fork; an example of saddlemaking art at its best with some gleaming silver trim to set it off. He was going upriver to camp and to gather cattle all alone for a big ranch located just a few miles east of the mountains.

I camped a couple of miles up the valley from him that night. Next morning I rode back looking for some of my horses and came out on the edge of the timber as he was saddling a fine-looking black bronc. The horse was standing quiet enough, but the way he had his ears cocked it looked like he was going to blow up, so I stayed on the edge of the trees to watch. When the cowboy stepped up onto him, the horse went straight up and bucked down the sloping meadow heading for a canyon where there was a falls. That was as pretty a ride as I ever saw and when the horse was only a couple of jumps from the drop-off, the cowboy swung his right-hand stirrup and slapped him over the nose with the long *tapaderos*. The horse seemed to turn back under his hind foot as he swapped ends and bucked back towards me coming to a stop only a few steps away.

I said, "Good mornin'! That was a mighty nice ride."

He grinned at me. "I didn't know you were here. This bugger can be playful sometimes about sun-up. Now we can go to work."

I never saw him again. Later I heard he had been killed in a Royal Canadian Air Force bomber raid over Germany. I have always wondered what became of that grand outfit.

Every bunkhouse and ranchhouse in the country had its

shelf where reposed saddle catalogues from various famous saddleries – Visalia, Frazier, Hamley's, N. Porter Company, Miles City Saddlery, Blake Miller, Bona Allen, Fred Mueller, Riley & McCormick, and Great West, just to mention a few of the many that operated in the U.S. and Canada between the mid-1800s and today.

For aspiring young cowboys, these catalogues were the most popular reading material. I recall perusing the Visalia Stock Saddle Co.'s attractive catalogues over and over in my early years till they were coming apart and being fascinated and covetous of the saddles illustrated there. There was also R.J. Frazier's catalogue showing some huge saddles with big square skirts and wide fenders. The fenders and side jockeys were lined with calfskin and some of them had thin rubber glued between to keep the horse's sweat from coming through. These big saddles weighed up to sixty pounds.

My father rode a pretty full flower tooled Visalia, a design that was exquisitely rendered in small detail. Its tree was made of box pine and it had small square skirts. It weighed only twenty-nine pounds. He was in town one day when someone sneaked into the livery barn and stole his stirrup leathers and fenders. He was one angry and disappointed man, very quiet and grim for a while. If he could have found the thief, that would have been one sorry individual indeed, but he never did. He got a local saddler to make him a plain set of leathers and fenders which he used for years. He finally broke the tree roping a cow and figured his saddle was finished. But my brother John and I took it apart, repaired the broken pieces of the tree with glue and wood filler, re-covered it with rawhide, and reassembled it. My father rode that saddle till he finally retired from ranching. I saw him rope and upset a big horse out on the range with it one day when he was over sixty and the saddle stayed together, so we must have done a fair job.

He bought me my first saddle secondhand when I was about thirteen. It was made by an unknown saddler, for he didn't put his name on it, only a number. It was made on a slick fork tree and by the looks of it it was an American saddle. The cantle was seven inches high and slightly bulged in front and was supposed to fit my rump. It was what is known as an eight-string rigging with the side jockeys separate and laced down at each end with a leather rosette under the ties. The forward rosette was positioned just right so when a horse bucked it rubbed me over the knee on the inside of my leg and many's the time I lost a strip of skin from this installation.

It was a good saddle for a kid to learn to ride in, for the pitch of the cantle forbade grabbing the horn. If I did, I was pitched over the horse's ears the next pump. If I rode by balance, and kept a close watch on the horse's ears, it was possible to stay where it hurt some but my pride wasn't flagged down. I rode that saddle for twelve years and thousands of miles, and topped off some salty broncs with it, before I finally traded it off for a secondhand form-fitter with round skirts, full flower tooled, made in Douglas, Arizona, by A. B. Egland. It was fitted with bulldog *tapaderos* lined in the toes with sheepskin, which were great in the brush anytime and especially on a cold, wet morning. But they were not much fun if a bronc blew up and I lost a stirrup. It was like trying to dodge a bucket hung on a rope. That rig was a good one for riding broncs, except for a seat that was about an inch too short. I was not very much in love with the "bear trap" design either, for while it made it easier to stay on top of a horse trying to kick my hat off, it could slow a man up for that split second needed to get clear of one that fell for one reason or another. It is one thing to sit on a horse and quite another to know how to get clear of one in a fall. Many men have been crippled or killed by a falling horse. One thing was very desirable about that old slick fork of mine: one could get out of it in about any direction in an instant.

One day I was riding a fine thoroughbred cross mare that was likely the smoothest-gaited horse I ever rode. She was sixteen and a half hands high, good on her feet, and fast. I was riding with a girl, travelling at a walk, side by side, along an old wagon road that was just two ruts in the grass. My mind was not on my horse and the mare was obviously wool-gathering too, for she put her front foot in a gopher hole, rammed her nose in the ground, and somersaulted clear over as quick as a flash. Without even thinking, I came off and rolled away from her to come up on my feet with my hackamore shank in my hand. The horse was lying on her head with her neck doubled back under her and my first thought was that it had to be broken, for she was motionless. The girl was sitting in her saddle looking down at my horse in utter horror, white as a sheet.

Then she saw me standing there and exclaimed, "My God, I thought you were under her!"

I grabbed my horse by the tail and managed to skid her sideways far enough to clear her head, then pulled her out straight with my hackamore rope. She rolled over, batted her eyes a couple of times, and got up to shake herself.

"Good as new," I said. "She must have a rubber neck!"

It was a good thing I had not fallen under her, for my companion would never have been able to move her and we were miles from the nearest help. Getting out of the way in such a mix-up is something learned through growing up on horseback. It becomes an automatic reflex but sometimes luck helps a whole lot.

I remember years ago moving a bunch of horses across a gravel highway out of one pasture into another. I was riding a little bay gelding that was as quick and surefooted as horses get. It was a nice June afternoon and I guess the horses, the pack string we used to take summer and fall visitors into the mountains, thought it was time to go for a trip, for when they went through the gate onto the road they turned down it heading for Waterton Park. My horse reacted instantly and was going flat-out in one jump to head them off when he broke through the sod into a badger hole with both front feet and instantly somersaulted. I must have gone maybe fifteen feet before I touched anything, then skidded on my face under the bottom wire of the barbed wire fence out into the ditch alongside the road. My wind was knocked out and I was slow getting up. On the other side of the fence my horse was just getting up with his wind knocked out too for he was humped up and his tongue was hanging out at full length. As I crawled back under the fence I was feeling lucky, for missing the wire was something to note, but I had also slid between two little piles of rocks left by the road construction gang.

By the time I got back in the saddle, and rode out to turn the horses back through the gate across the road, I noticed my shirt was red with blood down the front. Not only had I bloodied my nose but there was a generous slab of skin peeled off my jaw and cheek down one side. It was a reminder that nobody is indestructible and sometimes it pays to be lucky. If I had hit the wire or those rocks it would have been a different story.

The years of learning to ride bareback and then sitting that old slick fork taught me how to fall and to learn how to move fast in the right direction when a horse went off its feet.

Cowboys talk about a balanced ride and most give large credit to construction of a saddle for the proper position of a rider. It helps, but nothing will take the place of learning to ride with no saddle at all and then riding a saddle that is slick as a cow's ear.

Some of the best horsemen the world ever saw were the

old Plains Indians, who rode bareback long before they fashioned any kind of saddle, or even rode a pad of buffalo skin with the hair on, which was cinched onto their mounts with a surcingle, a band of soft hide that went clear around the horse. It was thus that they rode while killing buffalo with their bows and arrows and lances. And it was the way they sat their horses in battle against enemy tribes and in their wars against the white men. They were recognized by the U.S. military as among the best cavalry of the world.

CHAPTER 3

The Development
of Cowboy Costume

DON BRESTLER 93

The hat is the hallmark of cowboy character, for over the years it has been the most significant part of his gear – something that sets him apart from other mortals. The way it is worn, along with its shape, separates him from those who just adopt it for the looks of it.

The first big hats worn in North America were the Mexican sombreros made of leather, high-crowned and broad of brim, which had a built-in curl all around to stiffen it and prevent it from flopping down over the rider's eyes. Because it was nearly as wide as an average man's shoulders it was clumsy in the brush and wind, so they were fitted with a thong tied loosely under a man's chin. If it got knocked off his head, it rode on his back until such time as he could put it back where it belonged. It protected him from the sun and rain, but it was heavy – particularly when wet.

The sombrero and woven wool poncho were and still are

worn by Mexican riders. The poncho is a rectangular garment, with a hole in the middle for the wearer's head, made out of coarse handspun wool yarn with the natural lanolin oil left in it. It served as a rain garment, a wind breaker, and at night a blanket.

I once got acquainted with a little old Mexican when I wintered in Mexico about six hundred miles south of the border at the foot of the mountains near Lake Chapala. His name was Juan, his legs were bowed, and he had the wrinkles and colour of bark on his face along with black eyes that twinkled as though he was about to break into a laugh, which he often did. Juan was very poor, but it didn't bother him.

The weather in that high country was idyllic – clear, warm, and almost windless, reminding me of Kenya in Africa along the equator. It was too early for the rainy season, but in the latter part of January, it began to rain with a chilling north wind blowing. There was no fuel at the house I was renting and the place was dank and cold, when suddenly Juan showed up leading a burro loaded down with mesquite wood. As usual he was wearing a sombrero that made him look like an animated mushroom and a long, white poncho made out of angora goat wool. We exchanged greetings in a mixture of Spanish and English as he stacked the wood in the covered patio, and then I invited him to come in and have a generous drink of good rum to warm him up while I went for some money. He didn't stay long, but before he left it was very evident that the wool in his poncho had been clipped from a billy goat and had never been washed. The last I ever saw of Juan, he was weaving up the road, singing, with the burro walking along demurely behind him. I proceeded to build a wonderful fire out of that gnarled, dry mesquite wood and then to pour myself a rum. I hope that the blessed saints Juan was singing about took care of him.

The first American cowboys north of the border wore

hats made of wool felt. They were low crowned with a brim four to five inches wide. Wool felt tends to get floppy in exposure to weather and some of them pinned the brim up in front to keep it out of their eyes.

A man by the name of John B. Stetson got the idea of making felt out of coyote fur. The fur was an attractive colour, but proved to be too soft, so then he tried beaver, which was much better. In due course Stetson hats were synonymous with cowboy headgear from Mexico to Canada. Most beaver felt has varying mixtures of rabbit fur in it. The best hats have a greater proportion of beaver fur, hold their shape much better, and are more waterproof.

Stetson had a great name. They made hats in many styles, from conservative business types to one they called the Carlsbad, a big hat with a seven-inch crown and a five-inch brim. Most had felt that was clipped smooth, but the Carlsbad also came in unclipped velour. These were hard wearing and about as waterproof as a felt hat could be.

I remember one old cowboy by the name of Croppy, a tough sort of nondescript joker of questionable morals with a face like a prune, who always wore a big Carlsbad that looked like it had been recently run over by a herd of stampeding steers. One fall he was heading for the mountains with a local merchant who had hired him to guide him on a hunt. They had a short string of packhorses and Croppy was in the lead when they came to a young farmer ploughing a field and wearing a brand new, absolutely spotless grey velour Carlsbad, which Croppy looked upon with envy. The farmer was turning at the end of the field when Croppy stopped to visit while the packhorses and the hunter went on past. Croppy was admiring the hat with unabashed enthusiasm and its owner was pleased that it had been noticed. Croppy went to some length to assure him that it was about the finest hat he had ever seen, and wanted to know where he had got it. Then he asked if he could see it close up and the obliging owner got off his plough and passed it over the barbed wire fence separating them. Croppy duly turned it over and over admiring it from every angle before he took off his own old wreck and tried it on. It fit perfectly. Then he said, "I'll trade you!" and tossed his own over to the farmer, whereupon he spurred his horse into a run and disappeared in a cloud of dust. That was the last time the young farmer ever saw his new hat. For a while, Croppy looked almost respectable – even if he wasn't.

For a long time cowboy pants were shapeless and rough-cut but as time went on they took on style. Probably the first man to manufacture pants cut to the needs of a rider was Levi Strauss. They were made of blue denim, reinforced at the seams, low-waisted, and slim in the legs. Levi Strauss pants became a favourite with riders and are still a leading brand after over a hundred years.

Cowboys tend to be fashion-conscious and most of them will slip into the mode of wearing the best that they can afford. Probably the best western-style pants were those once made by the Pendleton Woolen Mills in Oregon. They were cut with an eye for style out of fine close-woven wool with the natural lanolin oil in it. They were medium brown with an open check in a darker shade, and some were fitted with soft buckskin wear patches inside the knees and on the seat. They were too warm in summer but were ideal for the rest of the year, being rain-resistant and almost windproof. They cost about ten times the price of a pair of blue jeans but would last for years. A short jacket to match was also available. A cowboy dressed in such an outfit was about ready for anything from a blizzard to a dance at the local hall. Many of Charlie Russell's cowboy paintings show at least one of the riders wearing these so-called "California buckskin" pants.

The Pendleton Woolen Mills are still making good clothes, but no more of these fine cowboy pants. Too bad.

Spurs and bridle bits have a very long history and came with the horses in the time of Columbus from Spain. The early Spanish cavalry wore armour and their hand-wrought iron bits and spurs were part of their equipment and were anything but delicate in design. No doubt they were used with care, for the conquistadors had limited numbers of horses of great value to them in the conquests. The first bits and spurs made by the Mexicans were very crude and heavy, the spurs having rowels four or five inches across. They were not as severe as they looked for they were worn on bare feet and the rowels turned easily, so when applied the points of the rowel came against a horse at a more or less flat angle. Bits were equally heavy with spade-shaped mouth ports and flat side pieces.

As time went on the skill of iron workers developed. The Californios' iron-forging along with their silversmithing grew into very fine metalworking artistry, though still very heavy. The Spanish spade bits could be cruel contraptions, but the riders' mounts were so well trained that the merest touch of the reins was sufficient. Most of the signalling between a man and his horse was done by subtle shifting of weight and pressure applied by a rider's legs. It must be remembered that those riders lived on horseback from the time they began to walk and were naturally very skilful in their relationship with their mounts. They had to be, for they depended on their horses for handling cattle, travel, sport, and about everything else they did outdoors. One historian describes a young Californio jumping his horse over a barrier while he balanced a silver tray loaded with glasses of wine without spilling a drop.

In 1968 I had a memorable experience in Santa Barbara

one day as I was travelling in a press car with a reporter I knew down a busy street past a new shopping centre. Out in the parking lot close by the front doors there was a saddled horse and a pack mule tied to an iron post with a big iron ring hanging from its top. A man was working near there making up a pack of groceries for the mule. It was such a curious scene that I asked my friend to drive in, so I could get a closer look.

The man was from another era. From his finely stitched boots to his silver-decorated sombrero, he was the living picture of an old Californio rancher. I walked up to him and introduced myself and he told me his name was Morino. He also told me that he had a small ranch in a pocket high up on the mountain above the city and every week he rode down for his groceries, something he had been doing for many years. When I mentioned that a hitching post in a parking lot was very unusual, he said that he had been buying his groceries at a store here for a long time, but when the owner tore it down and built this modern new place, he went to him and informed him that no longer could he do his shopping here. The owner of the shopping centre was very concerned for they were old friends and asked what was wrong.

"There is no place for me to tie my horse and mule," Morino told him.

The store owner smiled and told him to come back next week and he would find a hitching post waiting for him. I admired his outfit, for it was old but kept in beautiful condition. The saddle on his horse was of the old type with a big flat horn, and it was all flower carved and decorated with silver conchos and inlays. His bridle and reins and his *reata* were finely plaited rawhide. His bridle bit and spurs were silver-mounted works of art. He was, I guessed, about seventy years old but stood tall and straight with an air of dignity that was part of him.

By this time we were on friendly terms and I noticed that the top pack was cylindrical and hard, like a bucket of some kind in a burlap sack – a very awkward thing to tie down solidly on a pack. So I asked him if I could show him a hitch that I used for that kind of pack on my outfit back in the Alberta Rockies. For a moment he hesitated and then nodded. I guess he was a bit doubtful as I was dressed in a handmade western suit, polished boots, and a hat, and likely looked like a dude dressed like a cowboy. When I slung my hitch on that pack, it was there to stay, and he examined it thoroughly.

Then he smiled and said, "Bravo! A man is never too old to learn, *amigo*. This is new to me. I will remember it. *Gracias*."

The last I saw of him he was riding out through the traffic with the mule trailing close and the sound of shod hoofs ringing on the pavement.

Riding through timber, through brush and cactus, can be hard on a man's legs, to say nothing of his horse. The old-time Mexican *vaqueros* tied a kind of leather apron slung on a strap over the neck so that it hung in front of the horse's shoulders and came back far enough on each side to protect the rider's legs. But it proved to be too heavy and awkward so this design was abandoned. They fashioned leather leggings belted around the waist with an open seat. They called them *chaparajos*, which the cowboys of the southwestern states shortened to *chaps* (pronounced "shaps"). The first ones were shotgun style with the legs closed like pants. Then some were made with rings and snaps, which did not have to be pulled on over boots. These were called batwings because they had an outside flap hanging free – a common style still used. They could be plain or decorated with overlays of light leather of different colours. Both shotgun and batwings were also made of angora goatskin with the wool to the weather for riding in cold and rain. They were largely black or white.

Some of the batwing variety were white with black spots or orange with black spots. In later years another style of leather chap called chinks became popular. Shortened to reach just below the knees, and usually fringed, they are fastened down the side with thongs.

Over the years most cowboys have worn a silk scarf around their necks to keep out dust, provide warmth, and add a bit of colour. When I was just a kid some of the Métis riders wore a silk sash around their waists called a Mexican or halfbreed sash. Charlie Russell always wore one. On the northern ranges some men wore the old time *l'assomption* sash fringes woven out of wool, which were wide and generally scarlet with a fine design of black and white woven into them. Long enough to go around the waist twice and tied at the hip with a fringe hanging down, these were wonderful belly warmers in cold weather. Originally worn by French and Métis trappers and hunters, these sashes are collectors' items now and rarely seen today.

The cowboy's garb and various accoutrements have always been very distinctive, with a certain flair reflecting the character of the men who rode the plains and high country for a living, and ran from very plain to richly decorative depending on the occasion, location, and the man who wore it.

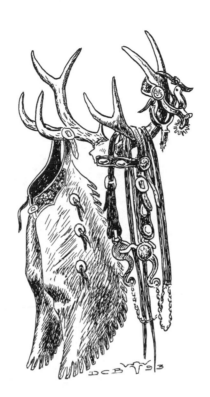

CHAPTER 4

Cowboys and the Buffalo

The early trail drives going north to the railroads from Texas encountered buffalo, which sometimes stampeded the longhorns and scattered them far and wide, causing losses. But the buffalo were on their way out of existence on the Great Plains, for the railroad was bringing in more and more people. As the trains travelled through the herds, they often slowed down to allow passengers opportunities to shoot at the buffalo, and of course there was no great effort to save the meat. The hide hunters systematically began to wipe them out for their skins, which were piled up in great stacks to be shipped east and processed into leather and robes. Nothing was done to protect the great animals, for the governments of both Canada and the United States knew that taking the food of the Indians was a sure way of subduing them. It was undoubtedly the most horrendous slaughter of its kind in

history, for close to sixty million of the big animals were wiped out between 1864 and 1877.

But there was a very small scattering of people who cared. Colonel Charles Goodnight, a wealthy Texas rancher, managed to gather a small herd which he kept on his ranch. Buffalo Jones, once a hide hunter, captured a few calves to start a herd. Colonel Sam Bedson, a Canadian in the Stoney Mountain country of Manitoba, had a herd of seventy head. Michel Pablo, a Mexican-Indian, and his partner Charles Allard, also of mixed blood, had thirty-five running free on their Flathead Valley range in Montana. There were a scattered number of buffalo owned by various zoos and individuals around the world. So in 1888 there was a grand total of 261 head of prairie bison left alive, most of them in North America.

Buffalo calves left motherless in the course of a hunt had a tendency to attach themselves to the hunters' horses. This was how Col. Sam Bedson obtained the start of his herd on the Red River not far from where the city of Winnipeg now stands.

In 1872, a Kootenai brave by the name of Walking Coyote was camping with a band of Blackfoot, probably Peigans, on the north side of Milk River not far from Writing On Stone in Alberta. Walking Coyote enjoyed acceptance by the Peigans, though the Kootenais and they were traditional enemies. This unusual circumstance was probably enhanced when he married a young Peigan woman who became his second wife. His first wife was a Flathead woman. The Flatheads were Christianized and the Fathers of the St. Ignatius Mission forbade plural marriage – indeed the tribe forbade marriage with a woman of another tribe. Walking Coyote's introduction of his Peigan wife into his lodge made for instant trouble. In the course of events there were a dozen or so buffalo calves wandering around camp with the horses. Probably thinking a present might placate his wife's people into taking him back, he cut eight calves out of the orphan buffalo among the horses. His Peigan wife suddenly rolled up her belongings and went back to her father's lodge, who naturally didn't complain, for he had the sixteen horses Walking Coyote had traded for her. Then for whatever reason the whole Peigan band packed up and left Walking Coyote and his Flathead wife alone on the prairie. He too packed up and headed back over the Rockies for the Flathead Indian Reservation with his buffalo calves. Whether he took the northern route over the South Kootenai Pass or made his way over the Marias Pass along the south fork of the Flathead is a hazy part of his history. But in due course he arrived with two bulls and two heifer calves at the Flathead headquarters of the St. Ignatius Mission. There he was given a good beating for his misdemeanours by the tribal police and eventually set up his lonely camp near Flathead Lake, a considerable distance from the Mission.

His buffalo thrived and in three years he had fourteen head. At this point Charles Allard and Michel Pablo made a deal to buy his buffalo, for two hundred dollars apiece. Walking Coyote took his money and proceeded to go on a prolonged binge that lasted for two years and ended when he died under a railroad bridge, unaware of the fact that his buffalo and their descendants would eventually travel back to Canada by rail from whence they had come to help re-establish prairie bison in that country.

But before that historic sequence of events occurred, the cowboys took a hand. Allard and Pablo had in the meantime purchased forty-four head of buffalo, including some hybrids (buffalo-cow crossbreeds), from Buffalo Jones, which he shipped by rail from Manitoba. Two years later Charles Allard died. Pablo took his share of the herd, after Allard's heirs had disposed of the rest, and turned them loose on his big ranch on the Flathead Indian Reservation. Pablo could not look after his herd and some were stolen by hungry people, but the remainder thrived. In 1904, he received notice from Washington that the Flathead Indian Reservation was due to be thrown open for settlement.

By this time he knew that his enjoyment of free range was over, so he approached both the American government and the American Bison Society with an offer to sell his buffalo. The Society had no money. The government dragged its feet, though President Theodore Roosevelt and Secretary of Interior Hitchcock were eager to make a deal. An agent was sent west to inspect the herd, who offered twenty-five dollars a head. Pablo laughed at him. He raised his offer to seventy-five dollars with a ten-thousand-dollar cut for himself, which Pablo indignantly turned down.

Pablo then approached the Canadian Department of Interior, asking about mountain buffalo range in Alberta, and had an immediate visit from the Commissioner of Dominion Parks, Howard Douglas, who offered an acceptable price for the entire herd. Pablo had no idea how many head he owned so the deal was struck at $250 a head delivered at Edmonton.

When this news leaked out to Washington via the press, there was a terrific uproar. Those good Americans who had been indifferent or actively obstructive to Pablo's original offer reached a great fervour of patriotism in their vociferous objection to the fact that the greatest buffalo herd in the nation had been sold to a foreign country. Meanwhile, Douglas arrived back in Montana with a contract, complete with a seal of the Canadian Department of Interior, to close the deal. Upon Pablo's signature being affixed, he was on the way to delivering his herd. How many he wasn't sure.

Because of the nature of his range, he still was a long way from delivery, for between his ranch and Edmonton was a round-up and over a thousand miles of railroad. With seventy-six of Montana's top cowboys mounted on the finest cowhorses, Pablo took charge. It was wild, rough country, with buffalo scattered through it that could run at thirty miles an hour, all with minds that thought of just one thing – escape. Time after time when it looked like a bunch was about to be caught, the wild ones stampeded and got away.

Charlie Russell, the artist, was with the crew for a while. In one of his illustrated letters to a friend he tells about trapping a bunch in a big corral built against a high perpendicular bank by the river. Upon shutting the gate on the bunch, the exhausted cowboys had supper and immediately rolled into their blankets to go to sleep. Come dawn, they sat up for a look only to find that they had one buffalo left in the corral, and it had a broken leg. During the night, their captives had tramped a graded trail up the bank to the top and vanished.

The whole summer was largely spent rounding up and losing buffalo. They even built twenty-six miles of fence leading from big wing corrals on the ranch to specially fortified pens at the railroad yards at Ravalli. Only a few buffalo were shipped out and Pablo was in the depths of despair. Some of the horses had been killed and several of the men injured. The survivors were exhausted.

About this time Charles Allard, son of Pablo's old partner, showed up. He was a devil-may-care cowboy with a lot of experience and a mind of his own. He contracted with Pablo to sweep his range of buffalo for two thousand dollars. With twenty handpicked men and 125 horses he went to work.

Young Charles Allard did not make any money out of this contract but he stuck with the job. Between June 1, 1907, and October 22 of that same year, Michel Pablo shipped two trainloads totalling 410 head. On June 3, 1908, another shipment of 190 head were loaded for Edmonton. After that the buffalo were caught in small numbers and put into adequate crates out on the range, loaded up in wagons and taken to the railroad stations at Ravalli. Canada received 716 head, the final shipment being completed in June of 1912. This is by long odds the first and most remarkable, and expensive, effort to conserve a species that was very close to complete extinction. In a speech made in the House of Commons, Prime Minister Wilfrid Laurier said, "Insofar as it is within the power of man, the buffalo shall not perish from the earth . . ."

At Elk Island Park the herd was looked after by a remarkable man, Bud Cotton, who with the help of a crew of transplanted cowboys proceeded to lend his talents towards thinking like buffalo. Elk Island Park was fenced, as was Wainwright Buffalo Park, where some of the buffalo were transferred. The herds flourished. At that time, the science of wildlife management was in its infancy. In spite of the slaughter of two thousand buffalo a year, the steady increase continued. The National Parks branch of Canada was in the buffalo-ranching business in a big way.

Today, there is a herd of about five thousand head in Wood Buffalo National Park, another thousand head in Elk Island National Park, and some scattered smaller herds, which are privately owned by ranchers and Indian reservations.

CHAPTER 5

The Last of
the Free Range

In 1882, the north end of the free range of Canada was just beginning to be taken up by settlers. It was known as the North-West Territories and encompassed the country reaching from Winnipeg to the Rocky Mountains, a vast sweeping stretch of prairies that was the choicest part of the Great Plains of North America, where the short buffalo grass lay curled as thick as the coats of the animals from which it got its name. Along its western rim, and in the foothill country of the mountains to the north toward the brush country, the buffalo grass gave way to bunch grass that grew stirrup-deep. All of this grass was unique in its propensity to cure on the stem so that it was little affected by frost and retained its food value for grazing animals during the cold months of winter.

Unlike the United States, where the settlers came ahead of established law, in Canada the opening of the west for

DON BRESTLER 93

settlement started with the arrival of the North-West Mounted Police in the late summer of 1874. The first thing the police did was close all the whiskey trading posts, a matter of making up the traders' minds for them, for the buffalo were getting scarce and there were few beaver and little of any other kind of fur left. Colonel Macleod would have liked to purchase the well-built Fort Whoop-Up from whiskey-peddling Fred Hamilton and John Healy but they couldn't agree on a price, so he took his force on west up the Oldman River about thirty miles where he camped on an island among the big cottonwoods. There the North-West Mounted Police built their own fort – Fort Macleod, the headquarters of law and order in western Canada. It was from this pinpoint on what was a vast expanse of prairie, foothills, and mountains that the Queen's War Hounds, as the artist Charlie Russell called them, proceeded to swiftly build a very profound and well-earned reputation among both the warlike Blackfoot Indians and the white men. Dressed in their navy blue uniforms from helmet to gleaming boots, with brass buttons shining in the sun, each man was armed with a .455 calibre Webley revolver and a .52 calibre breechloading Snyder rifle, and mounted on a big hunter-type Irish thoroughbred horse; they were impressive. There was not a man among them less than five feet, ten inches tall and most of them were six feet or over. About as physically tough as men could get, they were fearless but also fair, and they treated all men alike in enforcing the law.

When one American cowman drove a small herd of cattle into the valley of the Oldman River above the fort, he left a pair of pants on his wagon seat in camp while out riding with his cattle. An Indian came along and appropriated the pants, whereupon the cowman rode to the fort and stomped into the Commanding Officer's office to ask permission to shoot the Indian. The policeman pinned him in his tracks with a

pair of cold blue eyes and briefly informed him that if he shot
the Indian or anybody else he would be arrested and tried for
murder, and if found guilty would be hung by the neck till he
was dead. There was no further discussion.

It was this kind of firm, ungiving principle that very
quickly established the authority of the North-West
Mounted Police. They were few in number, only two hundred men, but big in their attitude. Any cowboy riding into a
settlement shooting his six-shooter off to get attention generally found himself facing one of the Queen's men who
would calmly appropriate the gun, and if that cowboy ever
saw it again, he was lucky indeed.

The first big herd of cattle to come to Canada from the
south came into British Columbia in 1860 with John Park
from Washington. He drove them up the Okanagan River
and on north up the great valley past the lakes, then over the
summit into the drainage of the North Thomson River
heading for the Caribou gold fields via Williams Lake, where
he swung north up the Fraser River to the placer mines. He
sold the steers to the gold miners at a good profit. These
were for the large part longhorns, with some crosses with
British breeds, the kind that the settlers had brought with
them by wagon trains across the prairies and mountains into
Oregon and Washington from the eastern states.

As John Park rode up the Bonaparte River in the country
around Cache Creek, he crossed miles of valley country
where grass up to his stirrups waved in the wind. He looked it
over again on his way back and decided it was a good place to
set up a ranch. So he headed south to gather another herd of
breeding stock. His ranch on the Bonaparte River a few miles
up from Cache Creek was the first in British Columbia. His
grandnephew, Gordon Park, still operates it.

Before the North-West Mounted Police arrived, the
Blackfoot Indians were still the power to be reckoned with

though their number had been depleted by smallpox. There were buffalo to hunt and their horse herds were numerous, but their sun had almost set. In 1874, the I. G. Baker Company had shipped a quarter of a million prime buffalo hides by steamboat east to St. Louis from Fort Benton on the Missouri River in Montana. In about six years there were very few buffalo left in any part of the Great Plains. When my grandfather, George Russell, arrived at Fort Macleod in 1882 with a government survey party from Ottawa, they killed an old bull close by the Cypress Hills about a hundred miles east of the fort. I recall him telling of seeing seven or eight buffalo on the south slope of the Porcupine Hills up the Oldman River about thirty-five miles from the police headquarters.

The Indians were starving and there were few cattle in the country to feed them. John and David McDougal had brought a small herd from Fort Edmonton up on the North Saskatchewan River south to Morley on the Bow River in 1871. In 1872 they went south and bought another hundred head in Montana.

By the time the buffalo had disappeared, there was a huge sea of grass with very little of anything to feed on it. When the Treaty of 1877 was signed with the Blackfoot, relegating the Indians to live on reserves, the Canadian government was bound by it to help the Indians, but there was no one in charge in Ottawa that knew how. As various settlers came into the prairie region with cattle, they had a rough time with the Indians, who were very adept at killing their beef and just as quick when it came to eating it. The police were having some worrisome difficulties handling the Queen's adopted children. The pundits in Ottawa proceeded to try to supply cattle to the Indians so that they could go into the cow business and raise their own beef, but the trouble was there was no cattle available in sufficient numbers and the Indians were very much inclined to just eat anything they received rather than herd them. Then they appointed a Member of Parliament from central British Columbia by the name of A. Dewdney as Indian Commissioner as the best man to handle western affairs. When he arrived in early July 1879, people at the fort were just recovering from a very bad winter and an epidemic of typhoid fever brought on by the carcasses of cattle that had died in the harsh weather along the river. The infant cattle business of the western plains had suffered much, and everybody was complaining about Indian depredations among their surviving herds.

Dewdney had seen roaming bands of braves desperately hunting for the vanished buffalo herds on his way west. When he got to the fort there were about five thousand Blackfoot camped around it hungrily and yet trustfully waiting for the government to keep its promises. They couldn't be blamed for sallying forth in small parties to kill a beef. When they did, they had scouts riding with them, and when a cow was shot the scouts kept a lookout for intruders. The dead animal was quickly skinned and cut into pieces. Every Indian grabbed a piece and took off for camp knowing that if they weren't caught with a branded animal on the ground there was no way they could be convicted of stealing.

Even when a charge was laid against them, it was not easy to get a conviction. On one occasion a white man rode up to a group of Indians who were obviously busy butchering an animal. He was literally standing over them before they saw him, and the cow they were butchering was obviously branded. He reported the theft, but when the case was tried in the presence of Commissioner Dewdney with Colonel Macleod presiding as judge, the witnesses for the Indians overwhelmed the cowboy's evidence to the point where the case was dismissed. This caused some heartfelt swearing among the ranchers and no doubt some smiles among the

Indians; they were learning fast how to deal with the white man's law.

There were two young Englishmen, Ted Maunsell and his brother George, who had taken up a ranch a few miles upriver from the fort. They purchased a herd of 103 cattle to stock their new ranch and moved them to it with great difficulty due to their inexperience. Finally, after much riding, they arrived late one evening at their corrals. Tired and hungry they went to their cabin to find the door open and the interior in considerable disarray. Obviously the place had been raided by hungry Indians and they were assailed by a feeling of real discouragement. But when one picked up the flour sack it was to find enough flour in the bottom to make a couple of batches of biscuits. When they looked at the nail where a side of bacon had been hung, there was a small piece left – enough for a couple of meals. If ever there were two young ranchers grateful to thieves, it was those two. The Indians had left enough food to keep them alive till they could get more.

The first round-up of cattle ever held in Alberta took place in early August 1879 in the vicinity of the fort, with a rancher by the name of Parker ramrodding the operation and sixteen very green men riding for him. They had a wagon, but the men were poorly mounted, some were riding mares with colts at heel, and they only had one mount apiece. Their supplies were so limited that they sometimes gathered duck eggs from the sloughs and boiled them hard to take care of those containing birds. For the large part these were eastern farmers, inexperienced, and about as green in handling cows as they could get. But they rounded up over five hundred head and branded the new calves, though it was obvious to all of them that there were a great many fewer cattle than the count of the previous fall.

Of the 103 purchased by the Maunsell brothers about

thirty days before, there were only fifty-nine left. For the most part the ranchers did not blame the Indians, but they very heartily cursed the negligent government and its Indian agents.

Meanwhile, Commissioner Dewdney had purchased supplies for the Indians for the I. G. Baker Company store at the fort, the only store in the region, which was supplied by bull teams hauling freight from their headquarters at Fort Benton. His purchases were very economic, for Mr. Dewdney was a very careful man with government funds, and while the Blackfoot were grateful, the goods were gone like magic. Dewdney was stingy to the point of bungling and was just as unpopular in his dealings with the white settlers as he was with the Indians. Had he been working in the United States, somebody would likely have shot him, but here he could count himself lucky for the restraint of not only the Indians but the white men as well and their collective regard for the Mounted Police.

The budding cattle-ranching industry on the Canadian prairies was running into many difficulties. The fall of 1880 was a bad one, with prairie fires burning off the range in many places. The worst one in the Macleod district was caused by an old trader, Fred Kanouse, who purchased a good-looking pony from an Indian. It showed some signs of mange, so Fred proceeded to rub some kerosene into its hide by way of treatment. Then he took his newly acquired horse down to the blacksmith shop on the edge of the settlement to brand it. As he pressed the red-hot iron against its hide, there was a sudden flash, and away went the horse burning like a torch across the prairie. Before the poor animal died it had set fire to a half-mile of grass. The fire almost burned out the whole settlement before it was put out by the hard work of every man available.

It was considered a very serious offence to start a prairie

fire and charges were laid against the erring Fred Kanouse. He was fined twenty dollars.

The Mounted Police had built a post on the Bow River about 105 miles north of Fort Macleod which they called Fort Calgary, the location being in the middle of the present-day city. It was kept in supplies by the I. G. Baker Company, bull teams hauling huge wagons, each one drawn by eight yokes of big oxen, and four wagons making up a train. Each brigade had a foreman and a cook. Oxen are powerful animals but they move very slowly at a plodding though steady walk.

How slow is well illustrated by the experience of Major Walker, a man who had come west with the first detachment of the Mounted Police and, after doing good work in Saskatchewan, had retired from the force. He was headed for Calgary when he rode into Fort Macleod, where he asked for his mail and was told it had left for Calgary two weeks previously by bull train. It had been raining and the low spots on the prairie were boggy, and to the Major's surprise, he caught up to the wagons at High River forty miles south of Calgary, crawling along at a snail's pace. The foreman told him that with any luck and some good weather he would be in Calgary in ten days.

Major Walker understandably felt that bull trains were too slow for mail carrying, so he proceeded to organize a mail service. He rounded up a good number of subscriptions at twenty-five dollars apiece, and made a contract for two trips a month with a newly arrived Englishman named "Lord Hugill" at sixty-five dollars a trip.

When my grandfather came to Fort Macleod in 1882 it was the end of a long journey by Red River cart from Brandon, Manitoba. He had trailed with a government survey party as part of their crew from Ottawa. A machinist by trade, he had worked indoors long enough to find out that it disagreed with his health, threatening him with tuberculosis, and his doctor advised him to go west to a drier climate. It was good advice, for by the time he arrived at the end of that journey he was in top physical condition, hard as iron, with all the makings of a real frontiersman. Perhaps it was his interest in working with iron, for about the first thing he did was to find his way to the blacksmith shop, where he found the blacksmith at the tag end of a horrendous hangover and very low in his mind. He had what amounted to a monopoly on a considerable business repairing wagons and gear for the I. G. Baker Company's bull trains. Apart from the big wagons, iron parts which wore out, and wheels which needed repairs, there were the chains running from the heavy yokes of each span of oxen back to the wagon. These often broke, so there were always chains to be fitted with new links, which he forged and welded from iron rods of the correct diameter. Besides that, there were shoes to be made and fitted to the oxen as well as to the police horses and work coming from settlers.

Old Smiley, as the blacksmith was known, could not stand prosperity; it worried him to a point where he proceeded periodically to go on a prolonged drunk that ended only when he ran out of money. It was at this kind of low tide in his life that Grandfather found him. Not only was his head aching, but his credit at the store had been suspended till he paid his bill. He was out of food and could not get the needed iron and other material to proceed with his blacksmithing. So when he saw this obviously green young man come into his shop, he naturally hit him up for a loan.

It was perfectly obvious to Grandfather that this was a good business and just as plain to him why the owner needed money. His experience in judging men was limited but he knew good blacksmithing when he saw it, and there was nothing wrong with Old Smiley's work – when he worked. So after some due considerations, he loaned Old Smiley some money, and got him to sign a demand note. Grandfather hadn't heard of the western way of sealing deals by a handshake and the blacksmith was in no position to argue about it. So the blacksmith shop was back in business and Grandfather left with the survey crew for the rest of the summer and fall.

When early winter came he resigned from his job with the survey and rode back to the fort, where he looked up Old Smiley to find him recovering from another drunk and in no way able to repay the loan. So he took over the business and hired Old Smiley to work for him, allowing him a part of his wages in cash and crediting the rest to the note. Together they proceeded to forge iron, and the old blacksmith was happy and stayed away from the bottle most of the time.

But he slipped once, with a comical result. One night he went to the local saloon where he apparently met some cronies and proceeded to get very drunk. In the small hours of the morning he staggered off heading for his cabin, but couldn't find it in the darkness. It was very cold and he finally found his way to the blacksmith shop where a banked coal fire in the forge generated a little warmth. Crawling up on the bench alongside a pile of bull chains, he fell asleep. After a while he began to get cold and reached for the blanket that wasn't there, but his groping hand found the chains, which he proceeded to pull across his middle. This operation must have been repeated several times, for when Grandfather came to the shop later in the morning it was to find Old Smiley still snoring with about two hundred pounds of chain piled across his body.

He dug him out and sent him home for the day. Old Smiley came back to work the following morning not much the worse for wear.

By spring, after a busy winter, Grandfather had his loan

back plus a fair profit, so he tore up the note and turned the shop over to its original owner. Then he saddled his horse and proceeded to go looking for a suitable place to make himself a ranch. In due course he rode out on the rim of the hills overlooking a lovely valley at the confluence of Pothole Creek and the St. Mary's River, about six or seven miles above the location of abandoned Fort Whoop-Up and eleven miles south of the new village of Lethbridge, now a city of sixty-five thousand people. As he sat on his horse looking at it, the folded hills and draws on both sides of the valley were green with the new sheen of spring grass sprinkled with wild flowers nodding in the breeze. Directly across the river was the Blood Indian Reserve. Seventy-odd miles to the west the solid phalanx of the Rockies stood gleaming with snow in a long jagged row of peaks against the faultless blue of the sky. The silvery rope of the river made a long lazy S bend with the creek running into it on the near side at the top of the second curve. It was an ideal location but somebody was ahead of him, for he could see buildings and a set of corrals beyond the creek at the near end of a long, almost perpendicular, bank about three hundred feet high. He could also see some saddled horses in the corral, so he rode down into the valley for a closer look.

The ranch belonged to a colourful character by the name of Paddy Hassen, a squaw man who had recently buried his wife, a Blood Indian woman. There were some questions as to the nature of her death among her Indian relatives, but nothing was ever uncovered to prove it was anything but natural. Paddy's hospitality was warm and he invited my grandfather into his house, who, in the course of their conversation, offered to buy him out. Paddy was willing to sell, so they arranged the details and thus Grandfather become the new owner of the ranch.

He knew the railway was getting close and, before he left

Fort Macleod, he had ordered a brand new Buckeye horse-drawn mower with a three-foot cutter bar and a one-horse hay rake from the I. G. Baker Company. He was aware of a demand for hay to feed the teams employed in building grade. When the new machinery was delivered to Lethbridge, he headed east with it along with a wagon, hay rack, and a team acquired as part of his deal for the ranch. Upon reaching the end of steel, he worked out an arrangement with the contractors to deliver hay at eighteen dollars a load, which was considerable money in 1883. All he had to do was go out on the prairie, mow the wild hay, rake it up in bunches and then fork it into his hay rack, piling it as high as he could throw it, and pack it down by tramping it. Then he hauled it and stacked it close by the survey line. When the weather was good, he could average a load a day and sometimes more. By fall he had a considerable stake.

Grandfather was on the move. Ever since he had left Ottawa to come west, he had been dreaming about a dark-haired young lady by the name of Isabella Bell whom he had left behind. The youngest of her family, with three tall older brothers, she was a very striking girl with flashing brown eyes, of medium height and stately bearing, well educated and with a keen mind. She could cook, sew, keep a neat house, and had all the other skills girls of that time were expected to learn, plus some other things like rowing a boat and handling a team of driving horses. She had learned about boats when her brothers went fishing on the Ottawa River. Horses were part of life for anyone who owned property in those days.

Grandfather had been corresponding with her and that winter he went east by rail. When he came back early in the spring of 1884, she was his wife.

That summer the railway reached Lethbridge, and she came west to join him on one of the first trains to reach that very new town. She rode the last hundred miles from Medicine Hat sitting on a plank laid between two sawhorses in the caboose of a construction freight train.

For some reason my grandfather was late to meet the train. Grandmother, nineteen years old, and fresh from the city, walked down the platform in her stylish long dress with the white and black ostrich plumes on her hat waving at every step. Leaving her pile of luggage with the station agent, she crossed the dusty street to the trading store. The place was full of Indians and when they saw her they covered their mouths with their hands in sheer astonishment. Then they crowded around her, so close she was frightened. But the storekeeper came to her aid.

He knew who she was, for he said, "Give me your hat for a minute, Mrs. Russell."

So she unpinned it and handed it to him, whereupon he took it to the other end of the store with every Indian following, their eyes fixed on those wonderful graceful plumes. In their own language, he told them about the feathers; how they came from across the big water from a huge bird as tall as a horse – a bird that did not fly but could run like a deer. They were deeply impressed and looked at Grandmother with awe as she pinned the hat back on when the storekeeper returned it.

"They never saw feathers like that, ma'am," he told her. "They think very highly of feathers and these are big medicine to 'em."

From that day forward, the Bloods called her Bird Woman.

Grandfather came with a team and a buckboard to gather her up along with her luggage and they drove out across the great prairie to the ranch. What her impressions were as they came out on the rim of the valley overlooking the river shining like silver ribbon thrown down between the hills, with the mountains lifting on the horizon beyond against the western sky, she never told me. Maybe she was a little scared as she sat on the wagon seat gazing at this immense lone land, but her back was straight and her head up as she looked. It was her new home. She would never regret that she came.

Bird Woman she was to the Indians and no doubt the moccasin telegraph was busy telling of her arrival as well as of her marvellous feathers. Occasionally some Indians came to visit and would be served tea as well as offered some small gifts that were always on hand for them. They called my grandfather White Shirt, for he always wore one. He made it very plain that when he was not at the ranch they were not to bother my grandmother. For a while the Indians honoured his wishes.

But one day, when she was alone, she took out some colourful braided rag mats and hung them on the rail fence in front of the house. There was a camp of several tipis across the river and no doubt they saw the rugs. She was sewing by the front windows when a party of braves rode up. A big brave, likely a sub-chief, got off his horse and proceeded to lift one of the rugs off the pole and throw it over his horse's back. She came out the front door with her broom in her hand and ordered him to put it back. He just ignored her and stood looking at her, his face a mask of imperious indifference. She told him again and when he refused to move, she whacked him soundly over the rump and pointed at the fence. No doubt he had never been struck by a woman before and, given the moment and the experience, he probably would have liked to have killed her for this insult. But her eyes were flashing and she showed no fear. Besides, he knew that if he laid a hand on White Shirt's woman there would be big trouble. After all, even among his people, she of the big feathers was well known and her medicine was strong. So he put the rug back in its place and mounted his horse. Among his braves there was some sign of smiles, while the people watching from the camp across the river must have been amused as the whole party followed him away and left her alone. It was a year or more later before any of the Bloods bothered her again.

Her mother had come out from the east to visit her at the ranch, and being a city woman she was no doubt appalled at the great sweep of country and its remoteness, to say nothing of the sight of wild Indians riding their ponies across the river flats. One fine summer morning they were by themselves at the ranch, when a small party of young braves crossed the river on their horses and rode into the yard. They wanted to talk to White Shirt, they said, which was likely not true, for they must have seen him ride away. Grandmother told them he was not home. Great-grandmother was terrified at the sight of these half-naked "savages" and wanted to hide in the cellar, which Grandmother refused to do. She chose to ignore them and they proceeded to hang around the yard, squatting on their heels and talking. This went on for several hours. Along about four o'clock in the evening Grandmother decided it was time to do something about them, for not only were she and her mother getting hungry for supper, but the cheeky teenagers made her a bit angry.

The horses were standing patiently with their bridle reins tucked under a driftwood log down by the river. She went out and began picking up bits of wood as though in preparation of lighting her fire, putting them in a fold of her long apron. Back and forth she went, while the Indians watched her. Finally she worked her way close to the horses and then she gave her apron a quick toss, scattering woodchips all over them. Naturally the horses pulled the reins loose and stampeded out of there heading for camp across the river, with the Indians *ki-yi*-ing along behind trying to catch up to them.

That was the last time any of the Bloods ever bothered her. Bird Woman and White Shirt were always friendly but firm and enjoyed the respect of the red men and women.

As far as I know they never locked the door of their house in their lives. Their quiet hospitality became well-known, for it was enjoyed by all who visited the ranch. My father was born in a little stone cottage in the small town of Lethbridge in February 1886, the first of six sons and a daughter. Most of them entered the world at the home ranch; some of them without even the help of a midwife.

I remember my father telling of one birth when he was about nine years old. The baby came sooner than expected, and was alive and well, but Grandmother was slowly hemorrhaging to death. Grandfather was unable to do anything for her and he sent my father on horseback in the dark of night to a ranch about six or seven miles away to get help. It was a lonesome ride but he finally saw a light shining in a window. The rancher hitched up a team and drove his wife as fast as possible to the ranch, where she was able to stop the bleeding in time.

My grandmother was a tough lady but the paramount quality in her character was dignity. She had a retentive mind with a marvellous memory for things she read as well as for times, places, and figures. She kept the books for the growing business and did it with her usual attention to detail. As a boy I recall her getting into an argument over some figures with her lawyer, which she won without any fuss, in a quiet way that was very final and left him red-faced. I always remember her as a very beautiful woman whom I adored. My only regret is that I never got around to telling her how much I loved her, but somehow I am sure she knew. Indians and white people alike all respected her, even the rascals.

Two of the neighbours, one Dave Acres, and the other Tom Purcell, who had taken an early retirement from whiskey trading when the North-West Mounted Police came west, went into partnership on a ranch but got into a quarrel and split up. Dave Acres took up a homestead on Pothole Coulee several miles up the creek from the ranch.

My grandmother was making breakfast early one morning, while Grandfather was out at the barn feeding the horses, when a knock came at the door. When she opened it, there was the tall buckskin-clad figure of Dave Acres.

"Good mornin', Missus," he said. "I just shot Tom Purcell. Where's George? I want to give myself up."

"You what?" my grandmother asked in amazement. "Did you kill him?"

"Christ, yes, Missus," Dave replied matter-of-factly. "Deader 'n hell!"

When Grandfather came, he told Dave to put his horse in the corral, and they had breakfast. Then he drove the confessed killer into Lethbridge, where he gave himself up to the police.

If the two hard cases had not been bragging so much about how they were going to kill each other at the first opportunity, Dave would likely have got off on a plea of self-defence. He had been saddling his horse in the corral that morning when Tom Purcell suddenly rode in, obviously somewhat drunk, and attacked him with a heavy elk-horn quirt. Dave had been scared of Tom for some time and had a rifle cached behind one of the corral posts. Backing toward it, while he parried the blows at his head, he swung it clear, pointed it, and shot all in the same motion, wiping his assailant out of his saddle very dead indeed. As it was, he got three years for manslaughter, the sentence being served at Fort Macleod.

There was a rather amusing sequel to this story. While in jail Dave was put to work repairing, cleaning, and oiling police harnesses. Being a squaw man, married to a Blood woman, he had lots of in-law relatives who often came to visit him. Whenever the chance arose, he would slip them a piece of harness through the bars which was then hidden under their blankets. Then he would make another piece to take its place. When he was finally released, he had a fine four-horse set of harness waiting for him, a caper which of course delighted the Indians.

My grandfather did not believe that fortune comes to those who just stand and wait. They were building a cattle herd and had acquired some horses. Every second year or so they added another son to the family, all healthy potential cowboys. The range was open to anyone with the livestock to feed on it. It was not all roses in the prairie garden, however; they both were concerned about the lack of school to educate their family. They solved this problem in due course by hiring as a governess a lady who had recently arrived from the east with her family. She lived with them and taught the Russell youngsters reading, writing, and arithmetic – the three R's as they were popularly known.

Grandfather looked at his horses, for the most part small, wiry Indian cayuses, about as tough as horses can get pound for pound, but too light for harness. He sent east for an imported hackney stallion and introduced him to his cayuse mares. The hybrid colts that ultimately arrived soon outgrew their mothers: big handsome horses that made great saddle and light driving animals with all the toughness of the native breed.

Every settler in the country mined his own coal from seams that were exposed along the banks of the river by the action of the water. It would burn, but was somewhat oxidized by the exposure to weather and water which made it smoky and filthy. Having done some prospecting up on the slopes of the valley away from the river, Grandfather sunk a shaft straight down in a likely spot in search of a mineable coal seam with the help of an immigrant coal miner from England. They found a seam of good clean coal. With some careful measuring and rough surveying of the angle of the slope, they dug another horizontal shaft into the slope below until they reached the seam. It was shored up with timber and fitted with some mining cars running on tracks out to a timber chute where wagons could be loaded. Thus coal mining was added to the ranch business.

As the country opened up, there was a big demand for heavy draft horses for the hauling of freight and farm work. So Grandfather contacted a Clydesdale horse breeder in the east and eventually received a stallion and several mares of this big handsome breed. Most bays, though some were black, they had white stockings with much feathery hair around their feet, were up to seventeen hands tall, and, fully grown, weighed close to two thousand pounds. A well-matched team of Clydes fitted with adequate harness looked mighty handsome hitched to a big wagon with red wheels and a green double box. They were longer in the leg than the Belgian or Percheron breeds and active as cats.

I remember Dad telling me the hackney stud hated the big Clyde with a burning passion and was always trying to get at him, so much so that they kept him shut in the corrals. But one day when everybody was at the dinner table, the hackney wound himself up and jumped the fence. The next thing they knew all hell broke loose out on the big flat in front of the buildings as both stallions squared off squealing like banshees.

There are few things in the world more fierce and final than a pair of fighting studs. Unless they are evenly matched, the death of one is almost inevitable. In this case the hackney was a David attacking a Goliath with almost half a ton difference in weight. If the big horse got hold of him with his teeth the fight would be short.

The Clyde was fast for such a big animal and had enormous strength, but the hackney was as quick as lightning. The big stud tried to strike but the little one gave him no chance to get close as they reared and struck at each other. When the Clyde tried to reach him with his teeth, the hackney whirled and kicked him hard on his front legs knocking him off balance. Whirling and squealing, they clashed and broke fast, the bigger horse always a little late in his lunges to bring those powerful jaws into action. Once, the big horse got his teeth into the hackney's rump, but the hackney kicked him hard on the shins so that all his opponent got was some hair in his mouth. Before the fight could proceed two riders came in from opposite directions, two lariats shot out, and the horses were separated with no real injury to either one.

By the time my father was sixteen, he was riding on the round-ups tallying the cattle wearing the 2G brand on their left hips as they were gathered and branded. He was very young for such responsibility, but he had been doing a man's work for some time and his age was no handicap among such a crew. He could rope and ride, had a good eye for cattle, and was no stranger to the prairie country, for he was part of it. He was a real cowboy in a crew of such men, for the Canadian cowboy had acquired all the skills of those from south of the border because quite a number of Americans had come north with their skills. Young Canadian men, along with those from Britain, who were moving into the west looking for opportunities and adventure, were not long in adopting the colourful dress and expertise of working cowboys. Naturally some were better at it than others. A round-up camp could find college graduates rubbing elbows with Texans, born and raised with cattle and horses, who couldn't write their own names. There were halfbreed Indians, scions of eastern North American society, and maybe a Mexican or two thrown in for good measure, but they all worked at the same kind of jobs, largely spoke the same language, dressed more or less alike, and generally blended into the cowboy culture. If some of them were green, they did not stay that way very long; learning was a matter of sheer survival. The best of them were found in the round-up camp.

There were two kinds of round-ups; the spring round-up where the cattle were gathered every day in a chosen region and new calves were branded the same as the mother. The fall beef round-ups were for gathering mature steers and dry cows for shipping by rail to market. Each round-up crew, made up of riders from various ranches, was commanded by a captain, chosen by the ranchers, who was in charge and also arbitrated any disputes that might arise regarding ownership of an animal. There could be twenty or thirty riders, each with eight to ten horses, a chuckwagon with a cook, and a horse wrangler whose job it was to keep the saddlehorses together and to drive them into the rope corral every morning at daylight.

One or two of the best ropers roped out the horses the men wanted. When these were saddled up, there were always some that bucked the kinks out of themselves and their riders, action usually accompanied by some cheering or raillery depending on the cowboy's ability to stay in the saddle.

Then the round-up captain took the crew up onto the nearest high ground and sent them off in pairs in various directions to comb the country for cattle. Meanwhile, the cook packed his wagon, hitched up his four-horse team, and headed out for a designated spot, and he was usually followed by the horse wrangler herding the cavvy. When they got there, a fire was built and the noon meal was prepared in time to feed the riders bringing the cattle. If the weather was hot, the men might take time off to have a nap, mend equipment, or do whatever else came up till mid-afternoon. Then the branding began, with a couple of chosen ropers heeling the calves and dragging them to the branding fire, where teams of wrestlers threw them, and held them down to be branded, castrated, and earmarked. As the ropers brought the calves in they called the brand of the cow that was its mother's and thus each ranch was able to tally their cattle. It was up to the various reps to see that their home ranch got fair treatment.

It was hot, sweaty, dusty work where a young cowboy received no favours for his youthfulness nor did such a youngster expect to be treated otherwise. He worked like a man, was paid a man's wage, and demanded to be treated like one as long as he did his job.

I recall a story Dad told of meeting a youngster only fourteen years old by the name of Elderidge, a tough, hard-riding, cheeky kid, who could sit a bucking horse or handle his rope as well as or better than most grown men. There was nothing retiring about him, for the chip on his shoulder was bigger than most and he would give some lip to anybody at the slightest excuse. The round-up captain ran out of patience one day. He and one of the riders tied the kid down to the wagon tongue and gave him a sound spanking with a pair of chaps – a punishment that stung his pride more than his bottom – and it did nothing but make him smoulder. The outfit was gathering beef and, coming in off his turn at night herding, young Elderidge sneaked into camp to slip his rope gently around the boss's feet as he lay in bed dead to the world. Before he knew what was happening, that worthy gentlemen was bouncing out across the prairie behind a running horse. The kid refused to turn him loose till he promised there would be no retribution. The boss didn't have much choice. He walked barefoot back to camp under a high moon gathering up various personal belongings on the way, while no doubt fervently contemplating murder. History leaves no record of the kid dying violently, so it can be assumed that he learned the virtue of keeping his mouth shut before somebody wiped him out.

The most important man in the crew was the cook. Most of them could put together a good meal cooked in Dutch ovens over an open fire. Some of them were artists who could bring forth fluffy biscuits that would melt in the mouth of a hungry man. Occasionally one would even find a way to make doughnuts, cooked in hot lard and rolled in sugar while hot and served as dessert for the evening meal along with stewed prunes. "Bear sign" they sometimes called them and most cowboys would ride miles out of their way for the chance to have a feed of them. Every chuckwagon had a small crock of sour dough for making pancakes, biscuits, and bread. It was a kind of frontier yeast culture put together with tender loving care by somebody with the knowledge and then kept warm and alive for years. There are records of the same batch of sour dough being used for over half a century. Every time it was used some was kept in the bottom of the crock and before it was put away more batter of flour and water was added and mixed to be ready for the next day. It gave a distinctive though not unpleasant sour-yeast smell to people who ate it regularly and didn't take a bath every day, which was just about everyone, there being no indoor plumbing in the country, much less in a round-up cow camp.

A routine day on the trail drive began when the cook rolled out well before sunrise to start his fire and put together a breakfast of cornmeal mush, steak or maybe salt pork, fresh biscuits, and coffee. Lunch was usually a biscuit or two stuffed in a saddle pocket at breakfast time, along with a handful of dried jerky. Supper was more steak or stew, sometimes alternated with Dutch oven beans, corn pone, or occasionally roots or greens picked up along the trail by the cook during the day. In season, the meal might be topped off with fresh wild berries and, of course, more coffee. A good cook could turn out tasty food even though the larder was limited. Meat was the main item, sometimes antelope, more often venison, but rarely beef. Killing a cow was something of a waste unless it was a yearling, for there was no way to keep it fresh for long in hot weather.

For some reason or other camp cooks can be very cranky and sometimes eccentric. If they were good at what they did, and most of them were, they were treated like fine china – very carefully, for nobody ever rawhided a good cook. Good food and lots of it was something every cowboy appreciated and one of the few real pleasures they encountered out there on the open prairie. It didn't have to be fancy – just tasty and plentiful.

Though noted for being crotchety and temperamental, these cooks were not entirely without a sense of humour. There is a story of one who was working in a remote camp one spring. The weather was very wet, and then got even wetter when a three-day storm blew in, and it rained till small creeks turned into rivers impossible to cross and even the coulees were swimming deep. Supplies were running low and about all he had left to feed the crew was beans. A hungry stranger showed up unexpectedly and asked if he could have something to eat. "Sure thing," said the cook. "We got thousands of things to eat – all of 'em beans!" Then he proceeded to ladle out a plateful from a big pot simmering on the stove.

While at family ranches the lady of the house usually oversaw and participated in the preparing and serving of meals, on larger ranches where a bigger crew was employed the year round, the cook was a part of it and almost always a man – sometimes an immigrant Chinese but more often a retired cowboy who through infirmities caused by accident or age could not hold down a rider's job any more. They had developed a culinary skill by way of following the only life they knew and retained a place on the payroll. It was a lot easier than working cattle while riding snorty horses in all kinds of weather. Most of them did a good job or else they didn't last very long, and some were superlative. All of them able to hold down such a job were treated with great deference even if they were as cranky as bears or as temperamental as opera singers. Nobody on a crew ever gave the cook a bad time intentionally, though sometimes when a horse blew up on a cold morning and bucked through the breakfast fire on a round-up, scattering pots and pans all over the place, everyone present was treated to some plain and classical profanity from the "kingpin" of the chuckwagon. It was a time when those that had been served breakfast ate it in silence and those that hadn't probably went without.

A top cook was usually famous far and wide, for the crew of his outfit never missed a chance to brag him up or give glowing accounts of his skill as a teamster. As has been said, it was always the cook's job to move the chuckwagon on from one camp to the next on a trail drive or a round-up.

My father told the story of how the foreman took the crew up onto the top of a butte at daylight one morning to line them out for the day's gather of cattle on a spring round-up.

Down on the flat below, the cook was up on the wagon just starting out for the next day camp, when all of a sudden the four-horse team hit the ground flat-out in a runaway. Swearing, the boss dispatched some riders to help get the team back in control before they piled the chuckwagon up in a coulee or washout. Their efforts to catch up were not aided and abetted much by the cook who was popping his long-lashed whip on each side of the lead team. By dint of some hard riding the cowboys rode in on each of the team to find the cook had somehow lost his reins, but they grabbed them up near the bridles and stopped the wagon.

They were sorting things out when the boss rode up to ask

the cook what the hell he was trying to do, wreck the outfit? The cook sat on his seat rolling a smoke as he let the silence sink in and then said, "About the time I started, a cross line broke at the lead team. I knowed that if I hung onto those lines, I was sure as hell goin' to do something wrong. So I threw 'em all away and took down my whip to keep those boogers runnin' straight."

Apart from some bedrolls that got bounced off the prairie no damage was done, but the cook's reputation as a real "skinner" didn't suffer any either. That story went all over the country fast and it is still going.

As a boy I heard another story about a round-up cook who had the reputation for being about as ornery as a cook can get. He was a very good cook, but he had certain set hours when meals were served and anybody missing them just went hungry. They were gathering beef on a fall round-up and one day, about an hour after lunch, a cow buyer showed up to take a look at the herd. The boss showed him around and then he asked if he could ride to the wagon for something to eat. Upon being assured he was welcome, he headed to where the wagon was parked and the boss went back to work. The cook saw him coming when he was still some distance away and when the visitor got there he found the gnarled, hairy old cook dressed in nothing but his battered hat and beat-up boots stirring a big pot of stew with the long barrel of a .45 Colt peacemaker as he eyed the late arriving visitor with all the promising malevolence of a cornered cougar. Not a word was spoken. The cow buyer just rode on past headed for town.

It was wild country, big and limitless in its expanses, with its share of eccentric characters. It was a place where boys grew into men in an inordinately short period of time and my father, Harold, along with his brothers, Frank, Andrew,

Ernest, and Fred, were not exceptions. Grandfather and Grandmother imbued them from birth with a strong sense of responsibility, fairness, and honesty, and the country taught them fearlessness but also a measure of caution, however small that measure might be. So they were part of the life of that big land getting a portion of their education from it as they grew through the experience of doing many things, much of it hard work but all of it challenging and sometimes thrilling adventure. It was a way of life nobody could encounter now, for the prairies, foothills, and mountains have changed. In those days there was not a barbed wire fence from the North Pole to somewhere away to the south. It was wild then and it was wonderful.

CHAPTER 6

Life in Cow Country

It was a huge land covered by an ocean of grass, where people worked with horses, either riding them or hitching them to wagons or buggies to get from one place to another. The wagons moved freight or livestock feed, and the buggies, which had springs and were generally drawn by light horses, and could be fancy and stylish with tufted leather upholstery, were used for quick travel across country to visit neighbours or to go to town.

It was in Lethbridge, Alberta, in Canada, that I was born in 1915. By that time the great ocean of grass that made up the Great Plains was divided up by barbed wire fences. The buffalo were long gone and so were the longhorns, but my father, Harold George Russell, who was the first white boy born there in 1885, had seen the prairie when it was still wide open, and had helped gather the last of the longhorns at the

DON BRESTLER 93.

round-ups with men who had ridden with the trail drivers from the south. He was the first real cowboy I ever met.

It was his stories of the old days on the range that had more than a little to do with my abiding fascination with cowboy culture and history. Raised on a cow and horse ranch at the foot of the Rockies, about eighty miles west of the old ranch taken up by my grandfather in 1883, with the smell of corral dust, saddles, cows, and horses in my nose, my memories of those days are keen. It is a nostalgic part of the later chapters of this story of cowboys, cows, and cayuses.

I recall my mother's buggy, given to her by my father for a wedding present. It was silver-mounted and well-sprung with hard rubber tires on the wheels. The harness was light with silver-plated buckles and snaps. It was a beautiful outfit, and with it a fast-stepping team could trot at about six miles per hour all day which, as wheels went in those days, was fast – much faster than a wagon drawn by heavy horses with no springs and iron tires on the wheels.

Because we lived with horses and worked with them every day, we had a great respect for them, looking after them and keeping them well-fed. A man who abused his horses or didn't care for them properly was held in very low esteem.

The land was wild, many of the horses were half-wild as the spirit moved them, and the early ranchers were some-times inclined to kick the lid off of boredom with a great bang of energy and let the pieces fall where they may. Dignified they could be, but most of them enjoyed handling high-spirited horses. Most of them enjoyed a joke, even on themselves.

The Maunsell brothers, mentioned previously, who established a ranch a few miles up the river from Fort Mac-leod, were an enterprising pair of Englishmen. Ted Maun-sell, the elder, was the better businessman of the two. Though both were good riders and not afraid of hard work, it was he who accumulated the land. He never did learn to tell one cow from another and totally depended on his foreman to take care of such details. His brother, George, eventually drifted away by himself, but Ted proceeded to put together one of the biggest ranches in the Fort Macleod country. As a sideline business, he set up a butcher shop near town.

One of his neighbours was an American by the name of "Hippo" Johnson, who had drifted north from the States driving a herd of longhorns. He was suspected of being very handy with his rope when it came to putting his brand on mavericks, but nobody caught him at it. He branded his cattle with a big O around a hip joint, hence his nickname. Hippo never missed a chance to badger Ted Maunsell with tricks that the Englishman always ignored with a certain dignity.

One morning Hippo was riding to town when he spotted a big calico-coloured steer wearing Maunsell's brand. He proceeded to drive it to Ted's butcher shop, where he put it in the pen at the back. The owner was presiding over the place alone while waiting for his foreman.

"Good morning, Ted," Hippo greeted him. "Come on outside. I just drove in a damn fine steer you might like."

When Maunsell went out with him to the pen Hippo conveniently manoeuvred the animal so its brand was out of sight against the fence.

"What's he worth?" Hippo asked.

"A prime animal," Maunsell observed. "Forty dollars is the going price. I could use him right now." Whereupon he led the way back into the shop and wrote Hippo a cheque. Hippo thanked him, pocketed the cheque, and rode away into town.

Later in the day, the foreman showed up and was surprised to see the fresh hide hung across the top rail of the corral fence and even more so when he took a closer look at it, for he usually picked the animals for butchering. He went into the shop and confronted his boss.

"How did you come by that steer?" he asked.

"Hippo Johnson drove it in," came the reply. "I needed a beef, so I bought it."

"You what?" the foreman roared. "You bought your own steer!" If there were times when the man weighed quitting against the comfort of a good job, this could easily have been one of them. He rode into town at a gallop looking for Johnson with much violence preying on his mind.

Upon finding that worthy at the bar, he somehow smothered an inclination to kill him on the spot. He labelled him for a thief with some additional smoky adjectives thrown in, which Hippo heard with an expression of injured innocence.

"I come across that steer a mile or so out of town and just drove him in. Ted admired him plenty and handed me a cheque. It ain't every day I get offered forty dollars for just showing a man one of his own steers, so I took it. But seein' as how you're so damn sore about it, I'll give it back."

He duly gave the cheque to the irate foreman and the pregnant hush in the place was broken by a laugh and then the whole saloon was rocking with mirth. It was another of Hippo's jokes on Maunsell and the foreman had no choice but to join in.

As a slave on a Texas ranch, John Ware grew up working with horses from the time he was old enough to ride. In his mid-teens he suddenly found himself free, able to go where he pleased whenever the notion took him. Tall for his age, very active and extremely strong, he was a superb rider who knew cattle, so it was natural for him to take to the life of a roving cowboy. Finding work was easy, but getting paid what he was worth was something else in a country just emerging from slavery. But he had a sunny smile and a quick mind and was always willing to take on any job. He was scrupulously honest and able to take responsibility. Life was still hard for a black man, but he survived. Fascinated with seeing what was over the next hill, he drifted from one job to another, gradually working his way north. Eventually he found himself in Idaho, flat broke and hungry, with only the clothes he stood up in, when he had the good luck to run into the Bar U crew.

Tom Lynch, foreman of the Bar U ranch west of High River, Alberta, was at Lost River, Idaho, the spring of 1883 buying cattle. He was short of men to move several thousand head of cattle home, when a big black man showed up dressed in rags and a cheerful grin asking for a job. At first Lynch was sceptical, but when John Ware proceeded to ride a snaky cayuse to a standstill, he got a job. When the new man proved adept at handling cattle besides being very good at getting along with men, he was promoted to trail boss of one of the herds for the drive. Thus John Ware came to Alberta to stay and become a part of history in that last expanse of open-range country in the west.

Ware found Canada to his liking, for the country had never known slavery and among cowboys a black man was judged by what he could do rather than by the colour of his skin. For John Ware, life was a round-the-clock celebration of freedom. Here was a man who had never known anything but hard work; it was his play. Laughter was always close to the surface in his make-up. Kindhearted, generous, and happy, he was just as likely to laugh at a joke on himself as on anybody else who was handy. There wasn't a mean bone in his body, but he loved to play a joke on others.

One day on round-up in the spring of 1883, he rode into camp to get a fresh horse, when he noticed the horse wrangler asleep in the bed tent. It was this man who night-herded the cavvy – the string of saddlehorses used by the crew – and brought them in at dawn every morning when the cowboys caught their mounts for the day's work. John saw his chance to play a joke. He stretched his rope across the front of the bed tent from a stake to the wheel of the chuckwagon. Then he began vigorously slapping the roof of the tent with his hands and yelling at the top of his voice for all and sundry to watch out for the stampede. The wrangler woke up from a deep sleep with a start, leapt to his feet, ran out of the tent, tripped on the rope, and came down with a crash flat on his face. All he saw was John and the cook doubled up with laughter. Of course, everybody in the crew had a great laugh about it and thought it was a huge joke.

But the joker, however entertaining he might be, puts himself in a vulnerable position, for there is always someone in a crew of men who waits and watches for a chance to play a joke on him. John Ware was not an easy man to catch off guard. He was a keen observer, a great rider, and absolutely tireless, but he had one weakness. He was deathly afraid of snakes, and one way or another somebody in the crew was aware of it. It was a fear that probably stemmed from when, as a boy, he had been whipped with a snake by his boss back in Texas. One morning when he left his saddle horse untended for a few minutes, somebody wrapped a small dead garter snake around his saddle-horn. When John took hold of the horn to mount the horse, he barely suppressed a scream of terror. Fun is fun, but he saw nothing funny about a snake – even a little dead one.

Fred Stimson was round-up boss that year and he and his friend George Emerson were sharing a small tent. The weather was good, so the rest of the crew just made their beds out on the prairie under the sky. A cowboy's bed is made up of blankets covered with a rectangular piece of canvas long enough to be folded over and under it. John Ware rolled his bed out not far from the tent, then joined the rest of the crew around the campfire. In the dusk of evening George

Emerson sneaked the coiled end of his lariat under John's blanket and took the free end into the tent.

When John went to bed, he was almost asleep when something moved under him. He froze and then the thing moved again.

"Snake," he howled as he came up on his feet running. His toe caught the rope stretched between his bed and the tent, and, scared as he was, he knew he was the butt of another joke. Fright turned to anger. With one sweep of his hand he flattened the tent and with another he snatched the covers off the two men, loomed over them like a mad bear, and grated out between his teeth, "Somebody goin' to get a beatin' fo' this!"

Fred Stimson came up on his feet with a gun in his hand.

"What in hell is the matter with you? Nobody hurt you. Go back to bed before this gun goes off!"

"Nobody done hurt me, only scared me half to death! An' Ah think it was yo, Boss. Ain't dat so?"

By that time every cowboy in camp was on his feet. One of John's closest friends took him by the arm and said, "Go easy, John. It was only a joke. Go back to bed and I'll put the boss's tent back up."

John did as he was told, but he didn't sleep. He was ashamed of himself and regretted his anger, but he was uncomfortable working for Fred Stimson after that. And somehow he was never quite as carefree again.

His adventures and experiences were many, but perhaps the most astonishing and significant of them happened one hot July day when he was riding for the Bar U. His horse was tired and thirsty when he came to a slough and rode into it to give the horse a drink. But the horse refused and began to paw at the water. Somewhat puzzled, John noticed a scum showing on the surface. Riding back to shore, he got down and looked closer. The scum was oily and smelled a bit like kerosene. He struck a match and held it close to the water, when suddenly the whole surface of the pond burst into flames. It was light crude oil that had seeped up into the slough from underground.

Some years later, in 1914, a well drilled not far from this spot struck a real gusher, the first oil well in what was to prove to be the first big oil field in Alberta.

John Ware homesteaded on what is now Ware Creek, a few miles northwest of the present town of Turner Valley, where he and his bride, Mildred Lewis, a black girl from Edmonton, proceeded with raising a family. He eventually sold his homestead and bought a small ranch near the town of Brooks, about a hundred miles east of Calgary on the main line of the Canadian Pacific Railway. It was there he died when his horse stepped in a badger hole and fell on him.

His funeral was held in Calgary and was attended by people from all over the country. One of these, a well-to-do rancher by the name of Sam Howe, intended to go to the funeral but his good intentions got sidetracked.

To Sam, whiskey was the juice to celebrate a happy event and to wash away the tears of a sad one. Sam was feeling bad when he bought his ticket to take the train to Calgary at Brooks. He sat down at the bar to wait for the train, but his private wake got a bit out of hand and his sense of direction twisted. He was sleeping on the train when the conductor shook his shoulder. "Sam! Wake up! Where are you goin'?"

"Where do you think I'm goin'? I'm goin' to John Ware's funeral in Calgary," answered Sam.

"Hell, Sam! This is the eastbound train. John was buried two days ago and we'll be in Medicine Hat pretty quick!"

That little piece of humour would have made John Ware roar with laughter had he been able to hear it.

Cowboy humour runs from the sublime to the utterly

ridiculous and more than one joke intended to die with a chuckle has proliferated and even boomeranged. A story is told about Seven U Brown, who was ramrodding a round-up near High River in the 1880s, when the green kid of the outfit asked one of the cowpunchers who the boss was.

With a perfectly serious expression on his face, the cowboy informed the kid. "That's old Seven U Brown, you'd better watch out for him – he shot his wife."

The boy was flabbergasted and after some considerable thinking about this dramatic revelation, he wanted to find out more, so he finally sidled up to Brown and asked, "Did you really shoot your wife?"

"Who told you that?" asked Seven U, whereupon the cowboy pointed him out.

Next morning when Brown was lining out the crew for the day's gather, he left out this particular rider who had enough good sense to stick with the boss and say nothing till he was directed otherwise. Seven U, riding a magnificent horse that day, made a tremendous ride without even noticing his companion. Arriving back at camp that evening, he turned to the cowboy sitting on his weary mount beside him and asked, "Are you hungry?"

"Plumb starved!" admitted the cowboy.

"Are you tired?"

"Dead beat!" came the reply.

"Good!" said Seven U. "That'll damn well teach you not to go around telling people I shot my wife."

When the great Matador ranch sold out its vast holdings on the Texas-Mexico border in the early 1890s to a Scottish investor, the deal was for all the land and cattle. But either some of the cattle were hidden in the brush or the original owners bought five thousand head, for it wasn't very long before the Matador was trailing north one of the very last herds of longhorns heading for the open range in the

North-West Territories of Canada. My father remembered
this big herd when it came into Alberta – a long, undulating,
seemingly endless line of cattle with their horns glinting in
the sun. They didn't find suitable range that was not already
being used in Alberta, so they turned east into Saskatchewan
and set up a ranch in the huge sweep of prairie northeast of
what is now the town of Maple Creek.

It was getting near impossible to drive cattle across country from Texas, for the country was being rapidly fenced and
the fees levied by the farmers for damage to fields of grain
was a constant and expensive aggravation to the stockmen
owning trailing herds. When the Wilkinson-McCord ranch
in west Texas sold out, they loaded their cattle, horses, and
equipment on eight big trains heading north to unload at
Billings, Montana. There they began a trek north, across the
border and on for about five hundred miles to Sounding
Lake, Alberta, arriving late in the summer of 1902. It was
long-grass country, where their longhorns thrived on the
bunch grass that stood up to their bellies, and for a while the
herds flourished and multiplied on range that was ideal.

But in the late fall of 1906 a blizzard struck with driving
snow and temperatures dropped to fifty degrees below zero.
There was no break in the weather; one storm followed
another and the cattle drifted, starving and freezing, and
there was nothing that could be done to stem the tide of one
of the hardest winters in the history of the cattle industry.

The buffalo, nature's wild cattle, now long gone, could
survive such weather, for they turned their big woolly heads
into the storm and worked their muzzles deep enough into
the snow to get to the grass. But cattle just turn their heads
south, maybe hoping to get closer to the sun, and nothing
can be done to stop them. Even if they come to some sheltered spot or an obstruction of some kind, they just pile up

and perish. The weather has always been the great unknown to ranchers and when conditions like those of the winter of 1906-07 hit the range country the only survivors were a few small ranchers who had put up hay in stacks fenced like barricades, and even then these owners lost cattle that joined the drifting herds.

Many years ago I talked to one old cowboy who grew up in the Sounding Lake country and remembered that winter of death. He told me of seeing one steep-sided twisting draw almost full of snow and dead cattle. One drifting herd after another got trapped in it to freeze solid in three separate layers. He said that for years afterward it was hard to ride across it through the piled-up bones and horns.

When the spring broke and the snow melted in 1907, the whole range was wide open again. Nearly all the big ranchers were broke, including the Wilkinson-McCord outfit and the Matador. Stories were common of men lost in winter storms and never found until the spring thaws revealed their remains. There were many epics of endurance recorded.

None could be more outstanding than one involving Bill Greathouse, a neighbouring horse rancher. By February, the whole crew of the Wilkinson-McCord ranch was down to just surviving, for they were powerless to do anything for their cattle with temperatures at fifty below zero and snow lying two feet deep on the level and much deeper in the low places. The ranch cook, a Mrs. Ellis, became dangerously ill. She was not only a fine cook but very well liked by all who knew her. Determined to help her, if he could, Bill Greathouse saddled a big grain-fed horse and headed for Stettler and a doctor, a hundred miles away.

The records do not tell what he was wearing, but he was likely outfitted with long woollen underwear, a wool shirt and pants, two or three pairs of wool socks, Indian-tanned moccasins inside overshoes, Angora woolskin chaps, a buffalo-skin or sheepskin coat, buckskin mitts with wool liners, and a fur cap.

Hitting a steady pace and keeping as much as possible to high ground where the snow wasn't so deep, he headed for the nearest ranch in line with Stettler. Upon reaching the place, he quickly told the people there of his needs and hurriedly changed his saddle to a fresh horse, the best they had. So he rode, changing horses four times on the way. Upon arriving in Stettler, he immediately saw the doctor, and while the physician was putting together a packet of medicine with instructions for its use, Bill took his horse to the livery stable, fed it well, and proceeded to take on a big meal for himself. Without stopping to rest, he then stepped back into his saddle and headed for home.

On the way back, he reversed the procedure, changing horses at each ranch till he came back to his own mount at the beginning of the last lap. He delivered the medicine in time, for Mrs. Ellis recovered. He made the round trip of two hundred miles in an astonishing thirty-six hours, through a vast, cold, snow-blanketed country, under conditions where landmarks were often invisible in the whiteout, and without hurting one of his mounts. It was an epic feat of sheer guts and endurance. Of such men the northwestern frontier cattle country was made. Bill Greathouse was big and tall as men go, but when heart and determination counted, he was a giant.

Not all of the cattle died that winter, for here and there a few big four-year-old steers and dry cows survived.

My father told of cattle that drifted south in such storms clear to the Missouri River from the Canadian ranges. Some of them then drifted as far southeast as the North Dakota badlands. By the time they were found they were getting fat again and they were rounded up and shipped on east to Chicago.

The Mexico ranch arrived at about the same time as the Wilkinson-McCord outfit, and by the same means. Wilkinson and McCord went north as far as the Red Deer River and established a headquarters east of where the Dinosaur Provincial Park is now located. It was owned by a British aristocrat, son of the Marchioness of Waterford, a family that could trace its lineage back to William the Conqueror. He was one of five brothers and, being an adventurous type, headed for North America where he set up two ranches in Mexico. He was known by all as Lord Beresford and, although he was labelled a remittance man, he was good at business, but had very little use for convention. His love partner was a black woman by the name of Flora Wolfe. Beautiful, loyal, affectionate, and shrewd, she did much to help build his fortune. Neither one of them made any bones about not being officially married.

Shortly after Beresford's two thousand cattle and six hundred horses arrived by rail, a Texas cowboy by the name of Hansel Gordon Jackson, better known as "Happy Jack" Jackson, came into the country with a shipment of cattle for Gordon, Ironside, and Faires big ranching company. He was an Irishman born in South Carolina or Georgia and grew up with cattle. He drifted onto the Mexico ranch in 1903, where Beresford hired him as foreman.

Tough and gruff, he ruled his cowboy crew with an iron hand, though he was fair and worked harder than any of them. Though buried deep behind his stern countenance, his sense of humour was strong, and he had a penchant for going on periodic drunks of enormous proportions and was adept at scaring the hell out of everybody by shooting flies indoors with his .45 Colt revolver. He must have had very specially constructed ears, for history makes no mention of his being deaf. Shooting inside a building is ordinarily a first-class way for anyone to damage his hearing.

Lord Beresford obviously appreciated Happy Jack's ability to get things done, as well as his eccentricities, for they were together for three years before Beresford got wiped out in a train accident while journeying between his farflung ranches. After several years of litigation by Flora Wolfe to lay claim to a fair portion of the Beresford property, she received an out-of-court settlement of modest proportions. She moved south to more familiar surroundings and the Mexico ranch was no more.

With all the cattle, horses, and cowboys gone, Happy Jack had nobody to swear at but the government, for when he filed for a homestead on the site containing the headquarters, he was required to pay $125 for the "improvements." "I built the goddamn thing in the first place," he swore, as is recorded by Ed Gould in his book *Ranching*.

Another chronicler of Happy Jack Jackson's life story, by way of a motion picture titled *Hell Ain't a Mile Off*, Michael Klassen wrote an article prior to the movie script which tells at considerable length of a diary kept sporadically by Happy Jack from 1908 to 1942, when he was found dead in his cabin at the age of eighty years.

Lois Valli, a neighbour, wrote: "It was very well known that Happy Jack drank a great deal at times, and who could blame him? He lived like a coyote, or worse. Though I think he did it because he chose to. Happy Jack was there on his own quite a bit you know. I think he drank from pure loneliness."

In a page of his diary written in his usual cryptic, humorous, though somewhat bitter way on the blank pages of Dr. Chase's Almanac, he left a record of his years in that big, lonely, semi-desert land which is salutary and very rare in western history, where the old-time cowboys played such a big part. He complained, poked fun at himself, directed pointed barbs at the politicians of his time, and damned the heat and cold and drought that beset him and his livestock there in the Deadlodge Canyon Badlands.

For instance, he wrote:

1909. Aug. 17 crossed cattle (over the river)
Aug. 18 Buck & The Kid Was Here
Aug. 23 Hot as hell every day
Sep. 5 Still Mosquitoes Plenty
Oct. 14 Blue Heifer Had a Calf
15 Worked Cattle Branded calves
19 Cowboys shipped
20 Cowboys Quit
Nov. 1 Branded Horses 13 Head
Nov. 15 8 Below Turned Horses out
Dec. 1 Mosquitoes is Played out

Another excerpt says:

1913. Apr. 20 Drunk
21 Drunk
22 Drunk
23 Drunk
24 Red Had a Calf 8 Days over
25 Still Drunk
26 Sick
27 Dam Sick
28 Worse
29 Very Feeble
30 Long Live Booze. Hurrah for Hell

The building of a railway into the area, the installation of a ferry crossing the river close by Happy Jack's cabin, and a flood of homesteaders all contributed towards taking away the prairie wilderness. The United Farmers of Alberta (UFA) government, the temperance movement, and suffragettes such as Nellie McClung, were all held responsible for his unnecessary discomfort. The vote for women was won and Prohibition took the bottle away from all, much to Happy Jack's disgust. He wrote:

> 1916. Mar. 31 No Booze this Month. Sounds like
>   Prohibition.
> 1916. Jul. 1 Prohibition Starts. Hurrah for Hell
> 2 Damn Drunk for Several Days
> 31 Damn Prohibition
> Aug. 3 One Bottle Thank the Lord
> 12 One More Bottle
> 27 Damn Prohibition
> Sep. 30 Good old Prohibition Still in Force
>   My Title for a Jug
> Oct. 26 Pretty Drunk cost $8.00
> 28 Drunk as Hell
> 30 Hurrah for Prohibition

People couldn't make a living farming in that country, as Happy Jack told them at every opportunity, and one by one they left until he had the country pretty much to himself again.

The latter years of the 1920s were tough and lonesome for him, but only a portent of what was to come during the Hungry Thirties when the Great Depression took hold. The hot winds blew up the dust in clouds hiding the sun at many times and buried the abandoned homesteaders' cabins up to their windows in great drifts.

His journal notes:

1931. Apr. 7 Cyclone all Day
9 Wind Wind Damn the Wind
17 Worst Wind Storm yet
27 The Ground the Bottles and all is Damn Dry
30 Good old Prohibition Days Wind Wind Every
Day.
1933. Jan. 31 Depression Still Here
Feb. 28 Hurrah for Depression Long May She Wave
Mar. 31 Long Live Depression Gets Worse
June 23 Hot & Dry God Damn the World by
sections

Happy Jack was not the only one looking for a way to improve things, and when William Aberhart came along with promises of better times via the path of Social Credit and a monthly stipend to all, he likely looked on with some hope. But when the Social Credit party swept the election, he was no longer so optimistic. In fact he rejected Social Credit. In an October 1935 newspaper interview, the old cowboy simply stated, "I don't believe 'em. This country isn't ready for fanatics to run its affairs." Premier Aberhart's wild promise of a monthly payment of twenty-five dollars in credit per month to every citizen of the province to cover their basic necessities never came to anyone. Where he once said in his journal, "My kingdom for bottle," he now wrote, "My kingdom for a basic dividend." His journal waxed satirical and sarcastic.

He was getting old, and when he sold his cows on June 23, 1938, he was truly alone except for a few horses he didn't bother ever to round up. In his last few years, his neighbours looked after him. Warren Fulton and his family, his closest neighbours, made sure that he had enough to eat and helped him all they could. When he died alone in his cabin after thirty-five years on the Mexico ranch, he left a legacy of a tough, unbending, lonely record of his life there – and his loaded Colt. 45 was near at hand.

His passing is a milepost marking the end of an era; he may not have done anything great but he survived in about as tough a place to make a living as there is in all the cow country of Alberta, where the winters are freezing cold and the summers are burning hot. Nobody lives on the Mexico ranch today and there is little left to mark its location except the weathered old cabin and some other buildings that show bullet holes where Happy Jack shot flies, and perhaps an empty whiskey bottle or two hidden in the weeds.

CHAPTER 7

Saskatchewan Campfires

The word Saskatchewan is an Anglicized version of the Cree word meaning "land of swift flowing rivers." To the south it is a great rolling prairie country, which blends into parkland to the north – aspen bluffs with rich grassland meadows – and this in turn changes to northern boreal forest dotted with lakes and muskegs. The prairies are semi-arid desert, scorching hot in summer and often as cold and windy in winter as the high arctic beyond the treeline. I have travelled across the Saskatchewan prairies in February under a cloudless blue sky when a ground blizzard blowing on a north wind hid the earth, and the whole world seemed one vast river of moving snow with only power posts and buildings showing that ground was still there.

When the early cowmen first saw the prairie, it was covered with thick, curly buffalo grass very nearly as rich with nutriments in winter as it was in summer; short grass

specially designed by nature to feed the grass eaters and to keep the wind from blowing away the soil that nurtured it. Those first ranchers were the toughest of the tough, hardened and tempered by the climate in an environment where survival of the fittest has always been the rule. The longevity of a range-bred cow or horse is shorter here than that of animals living in the long-grass country of the parkland, because their teeth wear out from sand picked up with the grass.

Many stories tell of hardships endured by people who have perished in winter blizzards so blinding that a man couldn't see his hand in front of his face. By contrast there are often summer temperatures of over a hundred degrees Fahrenheit – which makes for a temperature range of one hundred and fifty degrees through the seasons. It is a harsh land but beautiful too, a country where the eyes of people shine like those of hawks accustomed to looking at far horizons. Distances are part of this prairie country, where men who work there still think nothing of a thirty- or forty-mile ride or a hundred-mile drive to town for groceries and the mail. As in all big lonesome lands hospitality is an ingrained virtue, not only because the people enjoy company, but also because it is a necessity for travellers seeking food and shelter.

One of the best chroniclers of Saskatchewan history was the late R. D. Symons, an Englishman who migrated to the prairies from England at age fifteen in 1913 and stayed to become a top cowboy. His book *Where the Wagon Led* gives a graphic, well-written picture of what life was like then, along with a clear view of the country.

Young Symons, who was known as Charlie, was a long way from home when he made his way from England to New York to visit a relative and then headed west to Maple Creek, Saskatchewan. He was about as green as they came, but he had some advantages, for he had been brought up on a farm and so was no stranger to hard work. He loved horses, which he had learned to ride and work in harness. He had a long-standing dream to be a cowboy. On his first day in Maple Creek he had the good luck to meet Scotty Gow, a rancher who gave him a job at twenty dollars a month and board.

Scotty helped him choose and buy a suitable saddle, and some adequate boots and clothes before they set out by team and buggy for the ranch thirty-five miles away. He was not a young man any more, but he was highly respected by all who knew him. He had his brand XΛ (X Open A) on hundreds of cattle, and his horse brand, XA, on a fine bunch of Clydesdale draft horses as well as on a good number of saddle stock, some of which were for his crew and some for sale.

As they drove along the trail Scotty pointed out his brand on various cattle with details of the differences in the brands registered under his name. It was all new to Charlie and the old man was surprised and pleased to see his new hand making notes in a small notebook. This youngster was green for sure but he would not stay that way. He listened and he was not slow about asking good questions when he felt the occasion called for it.

When they reached the ranch headquarters, Charlie met Jake, the ranch foreman, an insolent individual who did not impress him very much, though he was careful not to show it. The rest of the ranch crew were away to the south working at the annual spring round-up of cattle with cowboys from the neighbouring ranches.

Jake was gathering horses and Charlie was assigned to help him. This took them many miles and Charlie found out that breaking in a new saddle was not all fun. By evening he was sore and was glad when Jake corralled the horses at a ranch where they stayed the night. Next day was more of the same, and now they were hazing a good number of mares

wearing the XΛ brand, most of them with new colts. They
also had a number of yearlings and two-year-olds, none of
which were branded. By this time they had covered more
than sixty miles. Again they stopped at a ranch for the night.
They had not gone far next morning when they met several
rough-looking riders who helped them haze the horses to a
set of corrals near a small store run by an unsavoury old character by the name of Geisner, who Charlie found was just as
mean as he looked. Geisner was also unwashed, and what
food he provided was scarce and not very tasty. Charlie was
not only tired and sore, he was ravenously hungry, but he
stuck to his job and kept his mouth shut.

When Jake and his friends proceeded to cut out twenty-
odd young horses, Charlie was forbidden to help them, but
he watched. As each horse was cut into a smaller corral Jake
proceeded to call their brands, but Charlie could see no
brands on them, which gave him some misgivings that did
not go away when he and Jake headed for home with the
mares and colts, while the other riders drove the rest in the
opposite direction.

Charlie was not reassured when he heard Scotty and Jake
arguing about something upon their arrival back at the
ranch. Next morning Jake wanted him to saddle a fresh horse
and go with him to round up more horses, but Scotty inter-
vened by saying he wanted Charlie to help him hunt for a
cow needed for milking. But after Jake had gone, he and
Charlie hitched up a team to the buggy and they headed for
town. There Scotty went straight to the Royal Canadian
Mounted Police detachment, where he arranged a meeting
with the staff sergeant. In a lengthy discussion, the whole
story came out. Scotty had been suspicious of Jake for some
time and had deliberately sent Charlie with him to gather
horses knowing that a green kid would be accepted and could
gather some valuable information. But it was too little and

too late. The young horses were undoubtedly in the United States by now. The sergeant questioned Charlie thoroughly and then dispatched two constables to ride out and arrest Jake, but he had disappeared and was never seen again. Scotty Gow had been too trusting and, as the sergeant admonished him, somewhat careless about leaving his young horses unbranded until they were two years old.

Like a lot of youngsters new to the country, Charlie was following a dream, and he was finding that somehow a lot of the romance in getting to be a cowboy was lost in long hours of hard work mixed with the generous helpings of real hardship that tested his endurance to the limit. But he stayed with it, trying hard not to make the same mistakes twice. Scotty, who perhaps had some reservations about his new hand in the beginning, watched quietly and felt considerable satisfaction. Charlie wasn't so green any more.

When winter set in with temperatures dropping, following a snowstorm about Christmas-time, to twenty-five degrees below zero and then on down to thirty and forty below, there was plenty to do. The winter camp up near the front of the Cypress Hills was close to some fine bench meadows where they cut and stacked the winter feed for the cows and weaner calves. The job entailed hauling the loose hay with a sleigh and a big basket rack behind a team of Scotty's fine Clydesdale horses to the ranch headquarters about seven miles away. This was Charlie's chore, one that took him all day almost every day to complete. Like a lot of people fresh from England, he found that the dry cold didn't bother him nearly as much as it did the rest of the crew.

In the face of hard weather, the crew had ridden out and gathered the cows and calves off the range to bring them to headquarters where the calves were separated from their mothers and put into a big corral with plenty of hay and water. Then there were the usual four or five days when the cows hung around, adding their protesting voices in a steady roar to those of their calves. The cows weren't fed, so it was only a matter of time before they wandered away to graze on the prairie. Every so often, though, usually at night, a cow would remember her calf and come walking back for a visit with her offspring. Next morning, she would be gone again.

That first winter that Charlie experienced, he got acquainted with the chinook wind. It could be far below zero for days, with everything creaking with frost, when there would be a sudden break with a great arch of black cloud forming across the western sky. Then the wind would come roaring from the southwest, the icicles on the eaves of the buildings would begin to drip, and soon the prairie would be bare again. That year there was mild weather during January and February, but in March there was an ominous hush, when during the day the sky in the north had a greenish tinge and at night there would not be a coyote howl or the hoot of an owl to break the profound quiet.

One day during this time Charlie was halfway home with a load of hay, when suddenly a blizzard hit on a driving wind from the north, freezing cold and full of snow. Soon he could barely see his team. They blew through their noses and, obviously thinking of their warm barn, broke into a steady trot. Next morning the wind was even worse, the snow so thick in the air that the men had to follow ropes strung between the buildings and the corrals. Fortunately, two of the cowboys who had been out moving the cattle to the winter camp got safely home before the blizzard struck. After that there was nothing that could be done but to wait and wonder how far the cows still out on the range would drift.

Charlie was due for some new experiences when the blizzard blew itself out. They were all busy digging snow away from doors and uncovering equipment when a cowboy rode in from the neighbouring East West ranch, to tell them that some XΛ cattle had drifted south along with some of theirs. How many there was no way to know, but he did know that they had gone through a gap in the hills toward Montana. Then, before the crew could do anything, it rained a bit, and then a switch in the wind brought back the blizzard and cold again.

It was impossible to ride, for the ice crust on the snow was like glass and could cut their horses' legs to shreds. So it was two more days before the crew could go along with their visitor from the East West ranch to look for cattle. The weather was warm again and the sky was brilliant blue, but the travelling was very slow. As much as possible they kept to high ground where the wind had blown the snow away, but when they had to cross low ground, their horses were belly deep and their stirrups dragging.

They began to find dead cattle. The first was a cow frozen solid standing on her feet in a drift; the only part of her in sight was her head, which the heat of the sun had bared so that she stood looking at them through dead eyes. It was enough to make young Charlie shiver. They rode out of the hills onto the plains, where more were scattered here and there among the drifts. Some were still alive, feebly trying to get onto their feet. The foreman was carrying a Winchester rifle and he shot them to put them out of their misery. At one place along a draw a two-year-old heifer came out of a hold under an overhanging bank of snow, instantly showing fight when she saw them. When they looked into the cave, there was a newborn calf.

They were joined by more riders from the East West ranch and the dismal search continued on horses that were dragging their feet with weariness. They stayed at the old McRae horse ranch that night to continue their search next morning. To make a long story short, they found five hundred cattle alive out of the eight hundred that had drifted with the storm.

World War One was blasting its way across France in a storm of mud, flying steel, and death. The young men of the prairies flocked to the colours until the ranchers had no choice but to make do with older men and boys too young to join the army. Charlie joined a cavalry regiment at age seventeen and shipped out to France.

His regiment served in transporting guns, ammunition, and supplies back of the lines, largely out of machine-gun and rifle range, but forever being shelled by artillery. But by this time, 1918, the German army was in full retreat with Allied forces in great trouble as they tried to keep up. The roads and most of the countryside was rank with the smell of dead men, mules, and horses – scattered among shattered buildings, trees, and mud in an awful array of destruction. Charlie's outfit captured hundreds of horses, many from the steppes of Russia, which the Germans had taken from the Russian army. Mostly they were useless since they knew no English, but Charlie rode one that was a good tough mount. When Charlie went by ship back to Canada in 1919, his body was still young but he was much older in his mind. He knew he was one of the lucky ones, for many of his friends were dead.

On returning to the Maple Creek country, changes were in the wind. Horses fetched a good price due to the demand from the homesteaders, although mostly they wanted heavy animals for farming. But even this market was threatened by huge tractors just beginning to show up on the prairies. For a while Charlie was in the horse-trading business, but he saw the changes coming.

When he was offered a job as forest ranger and game warden, he took it. This work put him on patrol through a huge area in the parkland and north to the boreal forest country. It was a free life on horseback, through a thinly populated area just beginning to be taken up by homesteaders.

He was riding through parkland meadows one day when he saw a thin column of smoke rising out of some brush by a little creek. Riding over to check it out, he got a look at a fine bunch of horses – a saddled horse and a packhorse close by a man crouching over the fire cooking his evening meal. It was Bill Greathouse, he of the famous winter ride made many years previously.

Like a great many others Bill Greathouse had been forced off his ranch during the drought when his horses were starving for want of grass. He just saddled up a horse, packed his gear on another, got behind his string, and drove them east into Saskatchewan until he found some grass. When it was gone he went looking for more, turning into a kind of nomad tending a fine string of about one hundred and fifty saddle horses. Once in a while he would sell one, but he always insisted on a price suitable to the occasion. This way he got the cash to buy his food.

He was all cowboy this one, from his fine handmade boots, California pants, silver-mounted spurs and bit, and top quality Stetson hat, to his handcrafted, flower carved Hamley saddle made in Oregon. His mount was always good for he had a big bunch to choose from.

Bill was not very popular, for his horses were always eating grass coveted by the scattered ranchers and homesteaders. When the complaining got too pressing, he and his horses just disappeared to show up somewhere else. Charlie was fascinated by him and took every opportunity to visit with him. Sometimes he would bring him a piece of venison, which was always welcome. So it went winter and summer for Bill. It was a tough life. Finally Bill died in a cold winter camp, and when his body was found, they also found a small roll of bills with a note that said, "Kase i kick the buckett, fix things up."

In due course Charlie met and married a girl. Like a lot of other people in the Saskatchewan and Alberta country during the depression, he migrated north and west in search of greener pastures and eventually acquired a ranch in the Peace River country in British Columbia. He was one of many immigrants from Britain, who came, learned, and quickly adapted to the ways of Canada's big open western country. He was outstanding, for he was a keen observer and he left a legacy in the books that he wrote recounting his interesting life.

CHAPTER 8

British Columbia Cow Country

DON BRESTLER 93

British Columbia, where nature's giants play, is a grand country of seemingly unending mountains, grassy valleys, steep slopes, big rivers, and great reaches of timber fading out towards the northern stretches of scrub trees and vast areas of scrub willows, birch, and tundra. Only about two percent of the province is arable land. Its climate runs the gamut from the dry semi-desert of the Okanagan Valley to the rainforest jungles of the region along the coast.

British Columbia has its own unique problems relative to raising cattle. Unlike the prairies, the grass is not good winter graze, for all of it north of Kamloops grows lush and thus freezes in the fall. Most of the grazing country is steep and high and subject to deep-snow winters requiring heavy feeding. Not many years ago, the only way many of the cattle could be taken to market was by trailing them overland, sometimes through long stretches of timber with very little

feed. Now they go by truck, which simplifies moving them but is still expensive.

Having travelled over most of this land, I am always impressed by its wildness in spite of the massive clear-cutting for its timber. When flying, riding, and driving over the vast reaches of its mountains and valleys, I have always marvelled at the courage, motivation, and pioneering spirit of those men who undertook the establishment of its early cow ranches.

The first white settlements were at Fort Langley at the mouth of the Fraser and at Fort Yale farther up the river, both Hudson's Bay Company trading posts. The Company also had another fort two hundred miles inland at Kamloops on the Thomson River. Though the records are hazy, the story goes that the first cattle came into the country by way of a couple of bold and adventurous men, John MacLeod and James Douglas, who brought some calves with them in 1826, when they took up land on the lower Columbia River downstream from what is now Trail.

When placer gold was discovered on the sandbars near Fort Yale, the find sparked some interest, but the gold was very fine dust, nothing like the rich discovery three hundred and fifty miles up the Fraser where the town of Barkerville was built. It was to Barkerville that John Park drove his first herd in 1860 to supply beef to the rapidly growing population of miners there.

These miners came from the overcrowded gold fields of California. Some of the first cattle that were trailed north from Washington State to feed this influx never got past Fort Langley, but others were trailed on up the Cariboo Wagon Road, which had been hacked out of the rock and timber by a hard-working contingent of Royal Engineers, through the Fraser Canyon to Spencer's Crossing, Ashcroft, Cache Creek, Williams Lake, and on north to Barkerville. Over this trail oxen, horses, and mules pulled and carried freight. One optimistic and ambitious Californian, who must have purchased a string of camels somewhere at a bargain price, arrived at Fort Langley, where he had no problem finding loads for them to carry to Barkerville.

A camel may be a big, tough animal, strong enough to carry twice as much as a horse or a mule, but it has a temper to match its strength. Designed by nature to live in deserts, camels were not very good at going up or down steep country, and boggy ground filled them with abject terror.

When a string of camels met a string of horses or mules on the Cariboo Road, what resulted inevitably was an instant riot with wagons upset and packs scattered from hell to breakfast. Horses and mules could get accustomed to most anything, moose, bears, and strange items they were required to carry, but they drew the line when it came to camels, and developed an immediate and chronic allergy to sight, sound, or smell of these high-nosed, arrogant-looking beasts. By the time the camel drivers had made a round trip or two, well larded with plenty of action on and off the road, there was much sincere and profane talk of shooting or hanging them. General epithets were so fervent and threatening that the owner decided to get rid of his camels, which was not easy. He did some promotion of camel meat at various overnight stop-over stations along the road, but nobody would eat the tough, stringy stuff. So ended the experiment with camels.

Beef, however, was in high demand, so it was only a matter of time before enterprising ranchers established cattle ranching in all the major valleys in the southern part of the province. The famous Douglas Lake ranch was founded by a group of businessmen in 1886 and today it has grown to 163,000 acres of deeded land plus a grazing lease. It was bought by "Chunky" Woodward in 1959 and runs about sixteen thousand cattle and two hundred quarter horses and employs a crew of forty-five cowboys.

John Park's Bonaparte ranch on the river of the same name, west of the town of Cache Creek, was not only the first real cattle ranch established in the province, but it was also the first to build an irrigation system to ensure sufficient hay for winter feed. Park employed a number of Chinese railway workers left stranded after the completion of the Canadian Pacific Railway to dig a canal diverting water from the Bonaparte River to his hay fields.

When I visited there about twenty-five years ago, I rode over part of the ranch with Gordon Park, grandnephew of the original owner. It was impressive country, but very steep on the slopes above the valley – so steep, I ventured to Gordon, that if his stock were to grow short legs on one side, it would be understandable. When I was there the irrigation of the hay meadows in the valley bottom was still being carried out by a Chinese family, direct descendants of one of the men who constructed the diversion canal with pick and shovel.

Another of the early ranches was founded by Norman Lee, a young Englishman, who also set up a trading post near the Chilcotin River west of Williams Lake. The market price for beef was high at Dawson City in the Yukon Territory in the late 1890s, so, along with a neighbour, John Harris, Lee undertook to drive two herds by the overland route north to the Yukon gold fields. No tougher trail could be found, for it traversed fifteen hundred miles of the most difficult country: big rivers, timber, and swamps where grass was soft and sometimes scarce and the problems unending. There was no hope of wintering the cattle along the way, which made the drive a race with cold weather.

Lee got to Atlin Lake, where he butchered his cattle, but then later lost his beef – some to spoilage and some in the wreck of the barge carrying it. Harris somehow got through to the Yukon River, where he butchered *his* cattle, and then proceeded to get frozen in the river ice two hundred miles short of Dawson City.

Word of the huge demand for beef at Dawson City got through to the prairie when Dominic Burns wrote a letter to Pat Burns, his brother, the famous rancher, whose headquarters were near Calgary. Pat gathered a herd of big four-year-old steers, put them in the charge of Billy Henry, a cowboy of legendary reputation, and shipped them by rail to Vancouver. Next they were loaded aboard a ship which sailed up the coast to Skagway, Alaska.

There Billy Henry jumped the cattle into the sea and they swam ashore. One story has it that they were then driven up over the Chilkoot Pass, a very difficult trail used by the prospectors, but in reality, upon scouting this route, Billy Henry knew it was impossible for cattle. The trail was strewn with the bones of horses that had died in the attempt to cross it. A few miles along the coast, Billy and his crew found an easier route that took them over the mountains to the Dalton Trail, which led them north along the foot of the Alsek Mountains and then northeast till they came to the Yukon River. At the Five Finger Rapids, they built big rafts out of logs, butchered the steers, and loaded their beef and horses to proceed down the river to Dawson City, where they sold the beef for seventy-eight cents a pound, and the hides for fifty cents a pound for dog feed. There were about fifteen hundred horses being wintered on two hay ranches in the valley, and a good demand for more among the twelve thousand miners, so they had no problem selling their mounts. Henry had lost some steers on his drive, but he got through with enough beef to make a profit.

A couple of years later he took another herd of retired work oxen over the same pass from Skagway to the Cassiar diggings in northern British Columbia and lost only one, drowned when it fell into a hole in river ice.

Billy Henry was not big physically, but he was all man, with a keen adaptive mind. I met him when he was in his late nineties. He was still active and mentally sharp as a razor – a real fine old-time cowboy. He lived to be 104 years old.

Even the Hudson's Bay Company had a hand in developing the British Columbia cattle-raising industry, for in 1892 they had imported about a hundred head, some of which they turned loose near their post on Graham Island, the biggest of the Queen Charlotte group southwest of Prince Rupert. Apparently their plan was to supply their various coastal trading posts with salted beef, but the cattle promptly lost themselves in the lush growth of the island's dense rainforest where they went wild.

A couple of Alberta ranches – the Gordon, Ironside, and Faires ranch as well as Pat Burns's – rounded up a number of them with the help of local Indians, but there was no way they could get them all. There were still wild cattle in 1935 on Graham Island.

My father heard of them and I wrote a letter to the Agriculture Minister in Ottawa asking for information, for we knew he came from British Columbia. He replied with a long letter saying that he not only knew something about these cattle but had taken up a homestead on the island in 1913, shortly before World War One. He said that he had been back to visit his homestead twenty years later to find trees twenty inches in diameter growing on the once-cleared trail between the beach and his cabin. Any ideas we had of rounding up the cattle in country where trees grew that big so quickly evaporated.

The huge Gang ranch was originally set up by Jerome and Thadeus Harper, two brothers from Virginia, along both sides of the Chilcotin River when the Barkerville diggings played out about 1867. Jerome died shortly after, but his brother proceeded with the development of the ranch. When his herds needed thinning out, he rounded up eight hundred big steers and dry cows and headed for Chicago. Going east he went by the trail to the Okanagan Valley and then south into Washington state and wintered in Idaho. In the spring he trailed them over the Rockies and east to Billings, Montana, where they were shipped out by rail to Chicago. The whole drive took eighteen months and whether or not he made a profit for his efforts is not known. What that trail herd ran into along the way while crossing big rivers and mountains must have been horrific.

But Thadeus Harper made another drive to Billings and then one by rail to California. It is too bad that he did not keep a journal. He died in Victoria in 1928.

The Gang ranch was taken over by an Englishman by the name of Thomas Galpin. At that time it was estimated to include nine hundred square miles of the Chilcotin area, most of it the wildest mountain and valley country imaginable. It is hard country with deep-snow winters. Cattle missed on fall round-ups could starve, but there also had been considerable rustling in these parts. Over the years it has changed hands frequently. It has always employed a big crew and, like most of the British Columbia ranches, it was made up mostly of native Indians who had adapted quickly to the cowboy skills.

Having heard of an outfitter and guide that had his headquarters on some lease land in the middle of the Gang ranch, Chilco Choate by name, and being somewhat homesick for a pack-train trip in the mountains besides being curious about that part of the country, I booked a two-week trip with him in August 1986, along with my friend Zahava Hanen and a Swiss couple, Sigfried and Nellie Bucher. It was wild and impressive country, very beautiful in its own distinctive way, with high mountains, lovely lakes, and clear, cold streams. In places the trails were among the steepest I have ever seen. Much of it was far from being cow country, but the valleys were grassy where we saw cattle. We must have ridden through a thousand cows with calves at heel and at least fifteen percent of the calves were mavericks, as unbranded cattle are still known. Obviously a lot of them had been missed when gathered for spring branding. In two weeks and at least a hundred and fifty miles of riding, we only saw about a third of the ranch.

The place has the makings of a first-class fish and wildlife preserve. It still has a resident population of elk, moose, deer, bighorn sheep, mountain goats, and wolves, as well as grizzlies and black bears. (I wondered if the bears would be blamed for any missing cattle come the fall round-up. Grizzlies have suffered considerably from being shot by the cowboys under the mistaken notion that all grizzlies are cattle killers. Bears readily feed on carrion and they tend to get blamed for losses not caused by them.) There are good nesting grounds for geese and ducks as well as a staging ground for migratory wildfowl of all kinds. The lakes and streams contain trout and salmon.

Whenever I travel the country that Norman Lee and John Harris trailed their cattle through heading for the Klondike gold fields, it has been with wonder at their sheer guts and bravery, for that is incredibly tough country. It is amazing that they got as far as they did under such exhausting circumstances involving big, dangerous rivers, mountains, heavy timber, swamps, and swarms of blood-sucking mosquitoes and flies. It must have been pure, unadulterated hell nearly all the way. Historically, it makes the old Texas cattle drives look like a picnic. But it all adds up to the amazing and enterprising spirit that has been the hallmark of the spread and establishment of North American cowboy culture.

CHAPTER 9

Trails of a
Young Cowboy

When I was four years old in 1919 my father bought a ranch about eighty miles west of the old home place south of Lethbridge and we moved from the prairies to the foothills. It was wild country where the steep rock of the Rockies came down within two miles of our door to a scattering of meadows and flats among groves of cottonwoods and aspens. It was there my brother John and I grew up. The ranch was fenced, as were all the other ranches, but to the west of us, the vast reaches of the mountains were free of barbed wire most of the way to the Pacific Ocean and north for two thousand miles or more to the Arctic coast.

There were few cars in the country then and we depended on horses. While we learned to work with cows, it was horses that we came to know best, for we spent most of our lives with them. We raised horses and Dad had a bunch of them ranging in the mountain country west of the ranch.

The horses were wild as hawks. They knew the country as well as the deer and mountain sheep and were about as indestructible as goats. We rounded them all up once or twice a year to brand the colts, castrate the young studs, and cut out those wanted for riding or working in harness. By the time I was fifteen and John was eleven, we were gathering that bunch by ourselves when they were wanted. Nothing could have been more "educational," for when you learn to trail, find, and then move the wild bunch out of such rugged country to the confines of a corral without having to backtrack and go through the whole process again, you have acquired what might be called horse-savvy. And there is only one way to get it – by experience. It was no place for the timid.

We would go west in the morning on grain-fed horses, make a swing across the slopes until we found some tracks, then work out their trail till we found the horses. This kind of tracking, where the sign could start off being several days old and rain might have partly erased the marks of hoofs, took some doing. We watched for droppings, which told us how old the trail might be, but sometimes in the spring of the year, the bears ate the horse manure while it was still fresh. I remember trailing five head once in June where I never saw a horse turd for close to twenty miles, though they were only a few hours ahead of me. A heavy rain had washed out most of the signs left by their hoofs, and bears had eaten their droppings. This was a time when thinking like a horse, knowing the country, and being able to see small things like fresh cropped grass and shrubbery were all that enabled me to finally find them.

When John and I located our bunch, they would likely be split up, so we were required to work out more tracks until the rest of them were located. If we were lucky we could get them all together by being very careful. It took very vigilant planning. We worked out our moves well ahead of time, for once we started them all for home they went at a dead run. Then we had to ride hard to keep them in sight, for if we gave them too much slack, they could vanish in the thick timber like so many elk and it would be all over for that day. Dodging snags, jumping logs, and detouring rocks we rode like the wind, yelling like a couple of wild Indians, heading off horses trying to break away from the bunch. In a couple of miles, we would have the edge run off them and it would be some easier, though those old lead mares, as sneaky as coyotes, left no room for a moment's carelessness. We never let up till the corral gate was shut on them.

For youngsters full of energy, it was something of note to get them all home. We took chances to be sure, but our horses were as surefooted as mountain sheep and generally we got away without a spill.

My favourite horse was Dad's big hackney-cayuse cross gelding called Chief. He had a deep ribcage and could run all day with a light rider, and knew what it was all about. Staying on top of him was sometimes a real challenge.

I remember one day running the bunch down a sloping meadow with willow clumps scattered over it towards a gate in a fence. The old lead mare suddenly swerved, heading the bunch for a deep coulee, and I swung to head her off. Chief was going flat-out aiming straight at a willow clump and I was set for him to jump it when he decided at the last moment to dodge it. I went over the willows with only one foot touching the saddle, all set for a hard fall, but Chief dodged back under me and I landed in the saddle again. Another time we were coming down a big ridge when the horses cut back under us heading for their favourite mountain. Chief swung straight down over what had been a snowdrift. Recently melted down to a strip of black mud left by pocket gophers working under the snow during the winter, it still had some frost under it. No horse could keep his feet in that kind of going and down he went, sliding with me still hanging on to the reins and coming along on the high side of him. He slid onto dry ground and I hit the saddle as he got to his feet. In one jump, he was going on the dead run again. We headed the horses and in another two or three miles we had them in the corral. All of me and one side of my horse was plastered with black mud but both of us felt real good.

I remember trailing along one time behind a bunch through snow in thick timber, wondering what had become of John. He suddenly showed up on the tip of a high bluff right over me against the sky. There was a big snowdrift all the way down from where he was sitting on his horse for about two hundred yards. He must have ridden out across old frozen snow on to fresher stuff, for suddenly the whole slope cut loose in an avalanche. He and his horse rode it down for a ways but then they got separated, and when the snow stopped, his horse was still in sight, but I could see no sign of him. I got off my horse and started to climb, but then I saw one of his mitts waving a bit as he fought to get clear. The snow heaved and he showed up wallowing down to his horse. We soon got things sorted out and took after the horses again. He had had what could have been a very bad experience but you would never have known it, for he had a big grin on his face when we caught up to the bunch. Snow sure helped with the tracking and trailing but it could be treacherous stuff sometimes.

It was a school of hard knocks, but we learned a lot in it. One thing I know for sure: nobody has really lived till they have run wild horses out of the mountains, and somehow we got away with it without any serious injuries. Sometimes now, I drive up into those mountains again, following service roads leading to gas wells that are sprinkled all over the once wild country. Just looking at those slopes we used to ride over going like the wind scares hell out of me. For a thousand dollars an hour, I wouldn't try it again. We sure worked our guardian angels or whatever spirits look after young cowboys in those great days of our youth.

Working with cows is usually a much different thing than with horses, but there are a few similarities. To do either one successfully requires thinking like the animal and knowing what it will likely do before it does it. Cow-savvy is just as important, only with cows you generally have to go slow. Working cows too fast is generally well-larded with utter frustration, for when cows get all steamed up and mad at the world, they are like pushing on a rope. Applying good cow psychology entails encouraging them to go where they think they need to go without letting them get the notion you might be working out the desired route. If a cow gets a notion to go some place, you just don't push too hard to get her to go anywhere else. You give her time to decide for herself – let her get the feeling it was her idea to change her mind in the first place. Cows aren't stupid, but sometimes, given the chance, they can be very stubborn animals.

I remember helping Dad with a bunch of cattle that we gathered to drive to the railway near Pincher Creek. We joined a couple of other bunches owned by neighbours and pointed them north, following little-used road allowance lanes fenced on both sides. Except for a crossroad and the odd open gate, it was just a matter of trailing along giving the beef a chance to water occasionally and feed as they went. It was slow and boring and come evening we were still about half a day's drive from the railway yards.

We had planned to go to a farmer's place that we knew for the night, but we had some grub and it was a warm fall spell of weather so we decided instead to camp on the trail not far from a spring in a nearby field, so we could get some water. The cows filled up and lay down and after a while we bedded down on our saddles with our saddle blankets for covers and went to sleep. I woke up sometime in the early morning, cold to the marrow of my bones. It was still clear but the temperature had dropped below freezing. When I sat up thinking about making a fire, I spotted a new haystack in a field close by, so I took my blanket and headed for it. Digging out a hollow at the base of the stack, I crawled into the hay. It was softer and some better but still so chilly in that sweat-dampened blanket that I nearly froze. I was shivering but somehow managed to drop into a fitful sleep. When I finally woke up, the stars were still out and I could barely move. Many times over the years I have slept out in colder weather, sometimes in snow, but never have I been so cold as I was that morning. My father was up, moving around a little fire making a pot of coffee. Everybody else was stirring and they were just as cold as I. We had some hot coffee and something to eat. The cattle were all feeding, and by the time we got our horses saddled, the eastern sky was lighting up. I'll never forget how good the sun felt on our backs that morning as we trailed on north.

Shortly after noon we came to the railway where a lane crossed the tracks a bit east from the yards at the station. There the cattle balked. They were mostly steers with a sprinkling of dry cows and they acted like we were trying to drive them over a cliff. Those two narrow steel rails were like a fence. We shifted the leaders and tried to cross them again and again. A train came along and that didn't help a bit. We waited till the rails quit humming and tried again. Then another train came along going the other way. We moved the cattle back down the lane to some heavy grass and let them graze awhile before lining them out to try again. This time Dad rode alongside the herd and dropped his rope over the horns of a big dry cow – a retired milk-cow. He worked her gently out of the herd and led her up to the lead, and when we came to the tracks, he let her stand till the rest of the cattle began to crowd up close. Then he took his dallies on the horn of his saddle and just walked her across behind his horse. A big steer followed her and then the whole bunch came across.

We were all happy when we closed the gate behind them and reined our horses around to head into town and to the Chinese restaurant. I was so hungry my belly was growling and that meal tasted mighty good. Dad went to the grocery store and bought a fat watermelon, which we ate in the shade of some cottonwoods down at the creek by way of dessert. Then we found the buyer and went back to the yards to weigh the cattle. For the kid of the crew, it was a long two days by the time we got home late that night. My bed never felt so warm and soft.

Sometimes trouble can show up when least expected. I remember many years later gathering a hundred and fifty yearling steers off the summer pasture of my ranch on the Cottonwood Creek and trailing them east to the Waterton River, where we threw them together with more yearling steers belonging to the Bennett ranch and Frank Marr's outfit. Yearlings can be touchy to drive and we were all feeling pretty good about getting them out of that brushy country close to the mountains.

We were heading for Park Bend, an auction ring and set of corrals at the end of a spur track not far from Hillspring with open-grass country and farms all the way. From up on point, where I was riding, four hundred and fifty steers looked mighty nice trailing in a long line. We had a good crew that second morning and arrived at the yards shortly after noon without a moment's trouble anywhere since we had started the day before.

Riding in the lead, I led the bunch up a fenced lane toward the yards, around the corner of the auction building, and headed for the open gate leading into the corrals. The cattle never missed a step and were right at my horse's tail when somebody inside the building started to hammer a nail into a board. Like a flash the steers behind me swung into a mill and I went with them to try to straighten them out. Frank Marr was with me and without any fuss we cut out thirty or forty head and again pointed them at the gate. Again came that hammering and again the steers whirled away. This time I rode over to the door of the building, reached down and yanked it open, and rode right into the place. A farmer was there with a hammer in his hand and by the look on his face, I knew he had been doing the hammering on purpose to spook our herd. I told him if he made another sound till we got those steers corralled, I was going to throw my rope on him and break him to lead.

On the third try we cut out a fresh bunch of steers and they went through the gate in a rush with the whole herd pushing them. They came within a whisker of going right on through the fence on the other side. The posts were all rotten and when the steers hit them, all that held them together were the planks that were nailed along their tops. If that fence had gone down, we would have had a real stampede and been gathering cattle out of farmers' fields for days. Wire fences and a stampede can be a real hummer of a mess. We sold our steers next day for a good price, so all's well that ends well. That was the last time we trailed cattle to market in that country. From then on, they went by cattle-liner. Another phase of the cattle-raising business was gone for good.

I always loved working with horses best. Somehow horses and the men that worked with them had a special aura of adventure that appealed to me.

When I was about fourteen my father gave me a little two-year-old filly that was pure cayuse. She was a bay with black legs and feet, and a white strip on her face, and wild as a deer. She was trim but had an ugly head with a Roman nose and sharp pointed ears. When she had her ears back, her profile was an unbroken arch from the end of her nose to the tip of her ears. But I thought she was utterly beautiful as I planned to break her to ride. I knew my limitations, and that if I was going to be successful I had to stay close to her while beginning to handle her. All of our corrals were too big. She would be able to take my rope away from me, which would not be good.

So I took my axe and went out into the bush, where I spent a couple of days cutting suitable rails and strong posts to build a small corral. Snaking these out of the bush with only a lariat and a gentle saddlehorse, I piled them up. Then I got them with a team and wagon and hauled them back to the corrals. For days I worked peeling my poles and posts, digging holes, and building a gate. When I was finished I had a round corral about seven feet high and a bit over thirty feet across.

Next morning Strip, as I called her because of the mark on her face, found herself shut inside of it all alone. She was nervous, and when I walked in with my rope in my hand she circled the fence. I stood in the middle watching her and not moving. She came to a stop facing me, but when I moved to build a loop, she again began looking for a way out. When I dropped a loop over her head and snugged it short close up to her ears, she went wild, rearing, pawing the air, and plunging.

Having helped Dad halter-break horses, I knew enough not to try to fight her by hauling on the rope but just kept the slack out of it until she was wet with sweat. In that small enclosure, there was no way she would get more than five or six steps from me, and she was getting all the exercise. Finally, she came to a stop, out of breath, her sides heaving, her eyes wild, and her nostrils open to the limit. Talking to her, I started towards her keeping the rope tight. Again, she whirled and ran, but by retreating a bit, I could play her like a trout on a line. Again she stopped and again when I tried to approach, she whirled and reared. This time I laid my weight on the rope, but she threw a front foot over it and jerked enough of it through my hands to burn me. Letting her have some slack, I waited till she stepped back over it and again put my weight on it. The loop of the honda was pointed down so that when I pulled it cut off her wind and she was frantic. She threw herself hard and rolled clear over to come up standing. Immediately I let her have enough slack to release the pressure on her windpipe and started slowly toward her. This time she let me get close to her before she plunged away.

We must have gone through that procedure a dozen more times before she let me up close. Moving from the side so she would have to turn a bit if she tried to strike with her front feet, I put out a hand very slowly and touched her jaw. She rolled her eyes and I worked a little slack in the rope to let her get her wind. She started to pull away, but I tightened the rope until she stood still and then I reached out and loosened the rope again.

She was a smart horse and it wasn't long before she realized that if she stood still, the rope wouldn't tighten on her throat. Now I scratched her sweaty hide and for a while I just stood talking to her. Then she put out her nose and touched my cheek. Stepping back very slowly, I pulled her to one side, making her take a step my way before slacking the rope. Soon she was turning toward me both ways every time I pulled the rope. It wasn't long before she began to follow me without allowing the rope to tighten. Gently I slipped the rope off her head, turning her loose. The first lesson was over. Opening the gate into the big corral, I put out some feed for her and left her there.

Next morning when I threw my rope on her, she blew up and stirred up plenty of dust for a little while, but when I laid back on the rope, she soon came to a stand facing me. And when I stood a step or two away with the rope still tight as I talked to her, she took a tentative step my way and then another. Immediately, I slacked off the rope and began to touch her gently around the head. It wasn't long before she was following me around the corral like a dog on a loose rope.

When I took the loop off her in the middle of the corral, she spun away and ran to the fence. But when I whirled a loop, she stopped and faced me. Walking toward her I held up the loop and told her to come. She dodged away, but I threw the loop over her head and laid back on her hard. She turned to come up to me, and I took the rope off. We went through that routine for a while, but it wasn't long before she just stood when I took off the rope. I could almost hear the wheels turning in her head, for in no time she was coming to meet me and putting her head through the open loop as I held it up in my hand. Once she spooked and whirled away. This time I stepped forward and whacked her smartly on the rump with the rope, ordering her to come. She came back and this time, after petting her, I gave her a little salt that I had in my pocket. Then again telling her to come, I walked away. She followed, and before long she was trailing around after me with no rope on her head. Lesson number two was over.

That evening I was sitting on a chair just outside the kitchen by the door, rubbing some ointment into the rope burns on my sore hands when through the screen in the door I heard Mother say to Dad, "I've been watching Andrew. Now that he's got that horse leading, he's going to ride her. It worries me. I wish you would start her."

"No way," Dad said firmly. "I've been watching some too – from up in the barn loft, when I should have been working." He chuckled and then went on. "He's learning, the filly's learning, and I've been learning watching them. The boy's got horse-savvy for sure. An Indian would say he's part horse."

"Part horse!" my mother exclaimed. "What nonsense! You watch close, hear me. I don't want him getting hurt."

When I slipped away to go to bed, I was walking on air. Dad was not given much to praise, but he had given me a great compliment that I would never forget even if I had reason to wonder once in a while over the years if he was right.

Next morning when I put Strip into the round corral my saddle was lying in the middle of it along with some other gear. For a while I talked to her and patted her. Most of the handling she had got was on the left side so far but that was going to change.

I slipped my hackamore over her head and then got a short piece of soft rope and hobbled her front legs. Taking a longer soft rope, I tied a loose loop around her neck with a non-slip knot so that it fitted back against her shoulders. Doubling the rope, I managed to snare a hind foot. She fought the rope a bit, but I pulled this foot up far enough so she had to stand on three feet. Tying it there with a hitch on the shoulder loop, I went for my slicker and dragged it up to her and all around her as she stood and snorted. Then I flipped it up over her back. She blew her nose and went up in the air, coming down on her side. When she got back on her feet, I stroked her and handled her all over, pulling her tail and talking quietly to her all the time. She stood trembling and sweating for a while, but then quieted down. Again I flipped the slicker over her back. This time she jumped a bit, but when I spoke to her, she stood. It wasn't long before I could flap the slicker all over her without her trying to move.

Then I went and got my saddle and slid it up over her back, adjusted the cinch to fit her, and pulled it up tight. She had a worried look in her eye and put her nose around to nuzzle me on the cheek as I untied the ropes. I walked her around for a while before bringing her to a stand, then, pulling my hat down, I slid my foot into the stirrup and eased up onto her back. For several minutes she just stood, but when I tried to move her, she suddenly buried her head and bucked into the fence, bumped her head and also my leg, then halffell as she turned. But she caught herself and threw me hard, knocking my wind out.

When I got some breath back and my eyes focused, she was facing me with rollers in her nose, chucking her head as though inviting me to try again. I walked over to her, gathered the hackamore reins, and again eased up on to the saddle talking to her gently. As before she just stood for a while and it was then I became aware of Dad sitting on the top rail close by the gate with a grin on his face.

She blew up again when I tried to rein her into a turn and I found myself up in a storm. But she couldn't really get going for she kept having to turn away from the fence. Back and forth we went with Dad cheering. "Hang and rattle, kid! Hang and rattle!"

Hang and rattle I somehow managed to do and when my horse came to a stop I was still on top. We were both reaching hard for our wind. After a while, I pulled her nose around in a turn and she began to walk around the corral in a circle. When I stopped her and slipped off, she nuzzled me as I unsaddled her, as though glad lesson three was over.

As I carried my saddle to the barn, I was aware of being pretty beat, but I wasn't limping. It was hard to limp when both legs were equally sore where the bark had got knocked off them against the fence. But I was standing tall, for though Dad didn't say much, I knew he thought I had done well. When we got to the house my mother looked at me sharply. She was an eastern girl, still not altogether sure she understood cowboys, but when she gave me a hug, I knew she was proud of me. As a matter of fact I felt real good about myself.

I had hung and rattled. To hang and rattle when the going got tough became a sort of personal motto that I have never forgotten.

The breaking of Strip proceeded from the corral to the ranch yard and then one afternoon I took her out for a long ride up on the slopes of the mountains, with my brother trailing along with me. She went for a couple of hours without a bad move. But when I caught a little dead tree in my stirrup and it broke off she blew up and bucked, but I managed to stay with her. Drywood Creek was running like a river with water from melting snow in the mountains. When I crossed, I lifted my feet out of the stirrups so I could keep them dry, when I got a horrendous cramp in the backs of both thighs. Had my horse even stumbled I would have fallen into the water. As it was, I managed to hang on, though I was in agony, and slid off her onto a dry sandbar, where I went to work on the seized-up muscles. When the kinks were out of them I rode back to the corrals knowing my horse was ready to go to work.

Strip was a natural-born fighter, though she never bucked again with me. She never got very big and stopped growing when she weighed about nine hundred pounds. She was one of the quickest horses on her feet I ever rode. I don't remember her ever falling. She loved it when I roped something and she was given the chance to play with an animal on a rope. Running loose, she liked to be by herself and was really cranky when she was in a corral full of other horses. She would quickly stake out her space. Let another horse enter it and she would squeal like a stud and fight them off. She was incredibly fast with her heels. Just how fast and hard she could kick, I found out one day.

About once a week, I would ride to town to pick up the mail and get whatever my mother might want from the stores. There was a big German shepherd dog that was not much loved on a farm alongside the road, a couple of miles outside town. He would sneak out to hide by the road when he saw a team or a rider coming, wait till it was close, and then attack viciously with a great roar. That dog had caused a couple of bad runaways, so I was watching. Sure enough, the dog came slinking into view and dropped out of sight in some tall grass growing in the ditch. My horse saw him too, for her ears came up and I could feel her go into a state of hair-trigger alert. She was travelling at a running walk and as she came to where the dog was hidden, she neither slowed down nor speeded up. When the dog launched himself at us with his usual barking roar, she kicked with the hind foot nearest him and her hoof made an audible crack when it hit. I turned to look in time to see his tail curl over his back as he rolled into the ditch, out like a light. Strip never turned her head or seemed to miss a stride but kept on at the same pace. I thought he was just knocked out, but when we came back, a couple of hours later, he was still in the ditch. He would ambush no more horses.

She never kicked our dogs, but she sure wouldn't tolerate a strange one barking at her. One time a couple of years later, John was riding her past a neighbour's ranch when three dogs came running and barking out of his driveway. Before John realized the danger, Strip kicked and killed one of them. He rode up the driveway to where he saw the neighbour standing and apologized.

"Those fool dogs know better than that," this owner said. "I'm sorry too. That was a good stock dog. Forget it. It wasn't your fault."

She was my first horse and one of the best I ever rode. Her feet were tough as iron and her hoofs rarely needed any attention other than a bit of trimming once in a while. She never knew what it was like to wear shoes. When I got a job at age nineteen riding rough string, guiding, and horse-wrangling on a big pack outfit owned by Bert Riggall, the internationally famous guide and outfitter, I took her with me.

His big half-thoroughbred horses were used to running in a bunch and undertook to put her in her place at the bottom of the hierarchy of their horsedom. One after another she took them on and it seemed I was always on the run to break up a fight. Sooner or later, she was going to cripple one of them, so I took her back to the home ranch. Dad bred her to a good saddlehorse stud and she got in foal. The colt grew up to be just about a perfect horse, a dark bay with black points and a small white star on his forehead. The only trouble was that he had no more sense than a box full of horseshoes. He knew how to sleep and eat, and go through a gate, but riding him was something to make a preacher swear. He was gentle as a kitten, had a great gait, and stepped out as though he was going to conquer the world, but if there was something to fall over or run into he would find it. I thought at first that he was blind, but there was nothing wrong with his eyes. He looked like a dream come true under a saddle and I kept him around the ranch for a while. Then one day he got tangled up in a barbed wire fence, cutting himself all to rags, and I had to put him down with my rifle. Strip never had another colt.

When I bought the pack outfit from Bert Riggall some years later, I brought her back to try her with the pack string again, but she hadn't mellowed a bit, so I put a little bell on her and kept her close to home as a jingle horse to round up the bunch in the mornings. In camp in the mountains she was content to stay close to the tents, rarely getting out of ear-shot. But when she put one of my best pack horses out of action by chewing a piece of hide out of his back, I traded her to an old cowboy by the name of Bud Jamieson for a nice-looking thoroughbred-cross filly.

I warned Bud not to put Strip into his corrals with other horses and I could tell by the look he gave me that he thought this was some wind up the creek. The first thing he did about as soon as I rode towards home was turn her into his corral with his team of big Percheron mares. He was eating lunch when the war started and he didn't even bother to look for a while, but when the squealing got worse instead of better, he went to the door for a peek at the battlefield. One of his mares was trying to find a way out of the corral and Strip had the other one cornered and was busy trying to kick her legs out from under her. From then on, Bud kept her separated. He rode her that fall gathering cattle and had a good time with her.

One night in late October it was snowing. Bud's homestead was just outside the boundary of Waterton Lakes National Park and had a corral built around a spring. It was made out of big logs with a hay yard next to it and a lean-to shed. Strip was in the corral alone when a big bull elk came down off the mountain and jumped in with her to help himself to some hay. Bud woke up to the sound of her squealing and fighting. When he lit a lantern to go out, the corral was suddenly silent. He found her down and bleeding heavily from deep puncture wounds where the bull's antlers had gone through her ribs. She blew the blood out of her nose and nickered, then gave a great sigh and died. When Bud told me about losing her next time I saw him, he was still feeling bad about it.

"She was little," he said, "but she made up for it in brave. There was no quit in her."

Horses are like people in some ways; there are no two quite alike. Some are leaders, most like to follow, there are some that like to work, and there's those that are as lazy as sin. I had about fifty that worked as a pack-train unit that ranged from leaders to a laggard or two who always insisted on being the "caboose" of the string when we were travelling. None of them was mean, for a pack outfit catering to city people with limited experience cannot be exposed to the kind that might hurt someone. Bert Riggall's outfit was started in 1907. I bought it after working for him for ten years in 1946. When I closed the outfit down in 1960, it had been going for fifty-three years. During that time of summer and fall use, wherein we had entertained guests from seven years old to seniors, we had not had one real injury – not one broken bone, which says something for good horses, management, and certainly for good luck. I had been the rough-string rider for a number of years and know a bit about luck, for apart from a sprained knee and some scars from hitting snags, I was never really hurt very bad. Except for a few years during the war, when business was slack, we were out in mountain wilderness country on expeditions of two weeks' to a month's length from June to October. Once in 1952 I left my headquarters on May 28 and did not get back till August 16 on a trip into the North Fork of the Flathead in southeast British Columbia.

I will never forget the first morning of my first real job working for Bert Riggall on his pack outfit. Nineteen years old and brimming with enthusiasm for the opportunity to work at something I really enjoyed in the kind of country I truly loved, it seemed too good to be true. We started out early that morning to round up a bunch of colts Bert wanted me to work over before the outfit was to head into the mountains, in ten days' time.

We gathered a bunch of sixteen fine-looking horses – big thoroughbred crosses weighing over a thousand pounds apiece. Nine of these so-called "colts" were five years old, and not even halter-broke. The other seven were all six-year-olds that had been ridden a little the year before and then turned out to pasture; one of the horses was eight.

Bert left me with them after he had introduced them, and I recall standing there in the middle of them wondering if I had bitten off more than I could chew.

That first day I halter-broke six of them. By suppertime my hands were cramping up to the point where I had to open one with the other to let go of my rope. I was about as tired as I have ever been.

The sixth bronc of the day was following me around the small round corral when Bert showed up to watch me.

"How many have you got going like that?" he asked.

"This is the sixth," I told him. "I should have the other three halter-broke by noon tomorrow. Then I'll start getting them broke to stand to be saddled."

He gave me a long look and then turned to look at the bunch in the big corral. Five of them showed sweat marks. I could see he was impressed, but he only told me to come for supper.

That was the start of ten days of unbroken effort to get that bunch ready for the trail. The weather was good, the horses were learning and so was I. What is really wonderful about learning is that there is no end to it. It just goes on and on. If a man can hold on to it, he can find out what it is to be happy, and being happy is what real living is all about. It never entered my head that ten days was not enough time for what had to be done with those horses. I just kept working at it, putting every fibre of my mind and body into the effort, trying to out-think each one as I worked with it, adjusting my technique to fit.

When I started to try out the half-broke six-year-olds, I picked the smallest of the bunch, a bay gelding that looked like he was all horse. He stood quiet to be saddled and I led him out onto a flat up Cottonwood Creek from the corrals. When I stepped up onto him, he promptly bogged his head and soared in a spinning jump. About the second jump, I made a grab for the saddle-horn and got a handful of grass right out from under his nose. He stood there with his head right over me with rollers in his nose as though inviting me to try again. The second try I stayed about four jumps before getting planted. Sorting myself out and getting my wind back, I stepped back in the saddle. This time I stayed through a session of the most crooked bucking I had ever known; at the start he never left a spot about twice his own length across. At first he spun to the left several jumps, then came out of it twisting backwards to the right before straightening out to go straight ahead. It was that backward jump that was the hardest to ride, and I was aware of a hind foot that was almost close enough to touch while his head was twisted around toward my opposite stirrup. Baldy, as I called him for the white spot on his nose, was an artist, and that first summer he bucked me off about as often as I rode him.

Frank Marr joined the outfit about the time we trailed the loose pack string to a camp about ninety miles northwest on the Oldman River just inside the Livingston Range.

Between us we kept those broncs working – when we weren't riding them, we packed them. We took our first party up the river to a lovely campsite on a flat where Slacker Creek joined it under the front of Beehive Mountain. It was a family party from Minneapolis with three brothers by the name of Stevens, and their wives and kids. We had forty-five horses, and between riding broncs, packing about two tons of gear when we moved camp, and keeping track of the bunch, we had our work cut out for us. Most working days were about sixteen hours and there were no days off, but we never gave it a thought. We had lots of good company in a magnificent mountain country, plenty to eat, and a comfortable camp.

There were tents for every two people, a stove for each of the tents, and no time to be bored.

When our trip was over at the end of three weeks we took our party to meet the Empire Builder, which ran from Chicago to Seattle on the Great Northern Railroad, at the station in East Glacier, Montana, and picked up another. So it went from June to the end of August. September and October was the hunting season, so the parties then were much smaller, four people being the limit. Besides being wranglers and packers, Frank and I were also licensed guides, so we worked under Bert to help find bighorn rams, mountain goats, and bears of trophy quality.

Bert's reputation as a bighorn sheep guide was worldwide. It had started back in 1910, when he took E. Phimester Proctor, the famous equestrian sculptor, whose big bronze statues still stand in a historic display in Washington, D.C., and New York, on a hunt in Yarrow Creek canyon not far from his ranch. He only had nine horses in those days and had to walk when he moved the camp up into this valley. On the third day of that hunt Proctor killed an enormous ram measuring over seventeen inches around the base of his horns. That was the way sheep heads were measured back in those days and, unfortunately, before record heads were measured on the curl, this head was lost, so where it would stand in present-day records is not known.

In 1924, Martin K. Bovey, a young hunter from Minneapolis, killed a ram with Bert up on Oyster Creek on the head of the Oldman River, which held the world record for many years and still stands second. Several other heads taken over the years by his clients were in the record class.

Back there in the fall of 1936, as a part of our work with horses, Frank and I were hunting under a master and there was no question of our enjoyment of the privilege. Guns and hunting being a big part of my life, I was particularly keen.

No stranger to mountains, I spent my days in one continual round of excitement. Frank and I took turns rounding up the horses after a candlelit breakfast in the cook tent, then we went out with the party for the day, and came back at dusk to round up the horses again before eating our supper, again by candlelight. We were getting lots of exercise and so were the horses. The rough string wasn't so rough any more. I remember some days that season when I rode three of them. By the time we came back to the ranch to turn them out on winter pasture, I made a rough calculation that my personal riding had taken me about fifteen hundred miles.

Riding the rough string came a lot easier. Baldy still bucked, but he always picked a spot where the footing was good with no rocks and logs. We came to an understanding the first ride out in the spring of the second year.

I never wore spurs with these horses, preferring to go slick-heeled. Part of it was for personal safety, for spurs sometimes get hung up, and part of it was because these horses didn't need a spur cue to move them. But when I got rigged up to top off Baldy that morning I wore a pair of spurs and tied them down. I also hung a shot-loaded quirt on my saddle-horn.

When I stepped up on him, he was facing the open gate of the corral and, as he walked out through it, it was easy to tell the storm would be coming when he hit the open flat.

When he bogged his head, I took a good firm hold on his belly with the spurs, and on about his second jump, I popped him over the nose with the quirt. He felt like he was trying to shed his hide for a while and the dust was flying so thick I could hardly see the ground. The storm was short but it sure was wild while it lasted. Baldy must have come to the quick conclusion that this was no fun any more, for he straightened out into a nice easy lope. He never bucked with me again for all the years I rode him, nor did he very often bump one of my legs when we were going through timber. He could get through the thick stuff behind a bunch of loose horses without missing a step or losing sight of them, which is a rare talent in any saddlehorse's make-up.

The only horse in the string that I couldn't train to ride was Jimmy, a big solid bay gelding with black points that weighed about twelve hundred pounds. He was the most punishing horse I ever tried to sit on. I rode him three times and the first two tries he threw me hard. The third time, I rode him till he quit, but I was as blind as a bat. He literally knocked me out in the saddle and if he had taken so much as another step I would have fallen on my head.

Frank and I decided he would make a great packhorse. The first time we packed him we had him hobbled with a long rope tied to the hobbles. He let us get the pack loaded and then he blew up. We grabbed the rope and piled him up on his nose, which he skinned a bit on a rock.

That was the only time he ever bucked with a pack through about eighteen years of working on the trail. Jimmy was one great horse who knew and loved the freedom of the mountains as much as I.

My life as a bronc rider, packer, guide, and outfitter over the twenty-odd years that I worked at it came to an end in 1960, when about every creek in the wild country I knew so well had a road running up it. There was no place left where I could take people to have the kind of wilderness experience for which our outfit was listed by various authorities as being one of the top three in North America.

For a while I thought of moving north into the Yukon Territory and setting up a business there, but when I went for a look at that beautiful, wild, big country, the thing that changed my mind was the very tough wintering condition for horses. The horses that were raised there could exist, for they knew the country well enough to find feed. They also knew how to fight wolves by bunching up with their heads together and kicking all hell out of any wolf coming within range of their heels. I loved my horses too much to subject them to that kind of strange environment. Besides, there were five youngsters and a wife depending on me by that time and the only schools worthy of the name were in White-horse – a long way from where I would be working.

It was time to change careers, so writing, photography, and cinematography became my way of earning my living. It was not easy, but it has worked out to be very successful and satisfying for all concerned.

Yet even today I sometimes wake up at night imagining I can hear the sound of the Swiss bells, hung around the necks of about every seventh horse, tinkling as they graze. Those bronze bells, each one playing a different key, made lovely music to a horse wrangler's ears.

CHAPTER 10

Tough Times

The Hungry Thirties were so dry that "the telephone poles were running around looking for dogs," as one old rancher put it. And as if the drought was not enough to survive, the economy was at an all-time low all over the world, with beef prices in North America down to a cent per pound – ten dollars for a thousand-pound steer alive on the hoof. There were lots of places on the prairie where the grass never grew enough to show green in spring; the dead grass blew away and then the soil drifted on the wind, even where sod had never been broken by ploughs. All over the Great Plains, people just abandoned their places, some trailing what livestock they had left towards the Peace River country, and some heading for the bigger centres like Winnipeg, Regina, Calgary, and Edmonton, where they joined the ranks of the jobless – thousands of them. Some went on the freight trains looking for work anywhere it might be found; others stood in

line every day for a ration of soup to keep from starving. All across the prairies, what were once prosperous homes stood abandoned and buried up to their windowsills in drift-dirt. Blinding clouds of dust often obliterated the sun so that at midday it was like evening and at night it was an unrelieved black. Springs and ponds disappeared. For miles and miles there were no animals but a few jackrabbits, antelope, and coyotes. Here and there bleached bones and maybe a few scraps of hide marked trail's end for horses and cattle. The hardiest survived and the hardiest were often the ranchers who, through geography and know-how, managed to keep a few head of livestock alive and somehow find enough to eat and wear to stay alive themselves. But at best it was a grim existence.

The ranchers along the band of foothills east of the Rockies had it best, for enough rain fell in the lee of the mountains to keep the grass growing even if the cattle and horses that ate it were worth very little. The banks that had loaned money to the farmers and ranchers foreclosed on land till they found themselves owning many thousands of acres with which they could not make a cent. Men like Pat Burns survived, for their cash reserves kept them in business even though profit margins were low. When it comes to making history, some people seem to be picked by the gods to excell in finding new trails, following them, and making dreams come true. Such a man was Pat Burns.

Burns was small in stature, but well built and fit with boundless energy and enthusiasm for his endeavours. Born and raised on a farm in Ontario, he ventured west with one of his brothers in 1880, first to Winnipeg, Manitoba, and then on by team and wagon to the country drained by the Assiniboine River, where they took up homesteads. They had very little savings, so Pat ploughed land for his neighbours and worked at logging for a sawmill in winter to gather some money. He got the chance to buy a small bunch of cattle, partly on credit, which he proceeded to butcher one at a time, peddling the meat at a profit.

In 1886 he got the opportunity to join in a contract to supply meat to the railway building camps along the route crossing the northern tip of Maine into New Brunswick. There he bought beef animals from settlers and drove them to the various camps. Many of the animals were work oxen, but in those times meat was meat and the jaws of the men who ate them were strong. Every daylight hour found Pat riding the country gathering cattle, driving them to where they were needed, and then going to look for more.

When that contract was completed Pat was offered another contract to supply camps in Saskatchewan, where a spur line was being built north from Regina to Prince Albert. Here the distances from the cattle ranches to the camps were greater, and there was very little shelter from summer heat and winter storms. But the ranchers were hospitable, offering Pat places to stay overnight. Once he was lost in a forty-below-zero blizzard. He stumbled on a rancher's cabin, where he was forced to stay for several days before the storm lifted. To offer to pay under such circumstances was unheard of and something of an insult, but when Christmas came, there was a big parcel full of treats for the rancher, his wife, and their kids, with a cheery note of thanks from Pat Burns.

When he set up his headquarters in Calgary, he built a butcher shop which was soon expanded into a meat-packing business. It wasn't long before he was buying hogs to be cured into smoked hams and bacon to supply the keen demand for these items over a wide area. When the packing house burned down, he proceeded to build another, bigger one, and outfitted it with the latest machinery and an expanded crew to run it. By this time there were many large ranches with thousands of cattle looking for a market. Burns's business grew till he was shipping Alberta beef cattle west, supplying construction crews across British Columbia and setting up butcher shops in mining towns along the railway and various spur lines all the way to Vancouver.

Pat Burns was a man with very little schooling, but he had a keen ability to judge people and to make the kind of connections vital to a rapidly growing business. One illustration of his entrepreneurial sense was the decision to ship a small herd of four-year-old steers by rail and barge to Skagway under the care of Billy Henry, when he received word of the demand for beef from his brother Dominic, who was in the gold-mining town of Dawson City. That successful drive led to another a year later, this time from Skagway to the Cassiar mining camp in northern B.C.

Pat was an astute businessman, always on the watch for a good deal, but never selfish in his dealings with people. Buying and selling cattle was his business, but he never forgot a favour, nor did he fail to offer help when it was needed in any community where he did business. He was a Catholic and attended a small church at Midnapore a few miles out of Calgary. One day he noticed that his church was being painted and it stood out next to the neighbouring church, which was also in need of paint. Very quietly, Pat Burns arranged a donation to cover the cost of a new paint job for it and soon both churches stood side by side equally shining.

As his business grew, Pat's travels took him to the nation's capital at Ottawa and across the Atlantic to London, England. He was the kind of man who was welcome in a homesteader's shack and in the mansions of royalty. When he married an English woman of aristocratic family and brought her back to Calgary, he built a mansion that became the hub of western Canada's society, where he entertained and conferred with leaders of commerce and government. By the First World War, Pat Burns was one of the wealthiest men in Canada.

He and his English wife did not have a very happy marriage, for he was essentially a cowman with the equivalent of a Grade 4 education, while she was a highly educated, cultured woman who loved good music and books. They didn't have much to talk about around the evening fire. Pat's appreciation of music was pretty much limited to the occasional hoedown in a one-room schoolhouse, where two or three musicians with a fiddle, banjo or guitar, and maybe a piano played for a dance. But he was a kind man and did his best to make up for his shortcomings. He would hitch a matched team to a fine rubber-tired buggy and take his wife for long rides across the country to visit some of his friends. He loved to run on foot and sometimes he would turn the reins over to her, while he ran alongside for a mile or two. Though he habitually dressed in a three-piece suit and wore a derby hat, he was a cowboy if ever there was one, and an athlete besides. When he mounted a horse, he reached up with his hand to grasp the horn and in the same motion vaulted into the saddle. Nobody ever made fun of his derby, which says something, for cowboys were prone to give wearers of such headgear a hard time.

He had always wanted land and bought several ranches till he was one of the largest landowners in Alberta. In 1928, he sold his packing business for fifteen million dollars, but he kept his vast ranches. When the King of England decorated him, he officially became Sir Patrick Burns, and he was made a Senator in 1931. He was highly honoured, but the same man, for neither wealth nor power ever changed him. There wasn't a cowboy in the whole country that didn't enjoy riding with him if circumstances allowed. He was a real giant in spirit and character, much loved and respected by all who knew him till the day he died.

Another legendary cowman was Rod Macleay, who owned a ranch in the Nanton area south of Calgary. When he left his home in Danville, Quebec, in 1898 to come west after a prolonged bout with rheumatic fever, his doctors told him that he might live for fifteen years if he found a place at a higher altitude. He found work on the ranches around the Highwood valley, learned fast, worked hard, and rode the same way. He was accused at times of being excessively hard-headed as well, but when the Great Depression came, he owned a ranch west of Nanton with a big lease of summer pasture on the upper reaches of the Oldman River between the Livingstone Range and the Rockies. Though he was heavily in debt, he hung on by sheer gut refusal to be beat and strength of personality.

Rod Macleay was a man who never subsided into gloom. He planted his feet and watched, for he figured there was no way the price of a thousand-pound steer could go any lower. If a yearling was worth only five dollars and a man could buy it, put it on grass and keep it till it weighed a thousand pounds, he would double his money. After all, the grass in the high country still grew, the rivers still ran downhill on their journey to the sea, cows still had calves every spring, and those calves became yearlings and those yearlings rapidly grew to weigh a thousand pounds if they got enough to eat. The only thing that held him back was lack of cash, but one day there came a letter from his bank manager with a summons to a meeting. Rod knew that the bank was planning to foreclose on his land. He did not waste time worrying, but instead saw the meeting as a chance to make what he knew was a good move.

He went to Calgary, where he made arrangements to sell

every head of cattle he owned that was fit for slaughter to his friend Pat Burns for the best price he would pay. He also bought himself the best hat and pair of cowboy boots he could find and, dressed in a good suit, complete with a diamond stick-pin holding his tie, and a gold watch-chain across his vest, he went to see his bank manager. Before that gentleman could open his mouth, he launched into his proposition with an engaging smile and no lack of energy or persuasiveness. The bank manager sat back and listened, accepted an invitation to go to lunch at the Palliser Hotel, listened some more, and when they finally parted, Rod had a big enough loan to buy a herd of yearling steers sufficient to graze his extensive holding of land. Not only did the steers do well, but when they were sold, the market had gone up enough for Rod to pay off a fair portion of his debt. When he died in 1953, well into his seventies, he left his two surviving daughters his Anchor P ranch, debt-free, along with a comfortable amount of cash.

He was not the only man who saw opportunity in the face of the greatest depression this country ever experienced; his was the same kind of positive courage that moved many others to do things that not only showed profit, but provided the kind of foresight and observation that benefited the land and enhanced the future of its people.

The fur trade was the foundation of Canada's economy, wherein the first Europeans spread out over the vast wilds of the north and west trading goods for the pelts of beaver, otter, marten, and other furbearers from the Indian, Inuit, and white trappers. Moved by the pressure of opportunity and greed, they overdid it by sheer plundering rather than careful cropping with respect for the country's ability to reproduce, so by 1880 the trade was about over except for a few remote areas.

But when the Great Depression assailed the economy

fifty years later, beaver were coming back and many other furbearers were in good numbers. Strangely enough, fur prices were good in Europe, providing a top market for pelts. A good prime coyote or mink skin would bring ten dollars – as much as a steer. To many of the ranchers and farmers, the opportunity did not register; they were not hunters or trappers and were too busy to learn. But for some, it gave them an edge on survival. In those days a hundred dollars would buy enough flour, sugar, dried prunes, and canned milk to keep a family over the winter. Fifteen dollars extra would buy a beef and a pig for butchering. Wild meat was free for the taking and if there was a root house stocked with potatoes, turnips, carrots, and onions, the living was excellent.

One bachelor rancher that I knew had a good rifle, a Model 99 Savage .250 calibre, with which he gathered coyote skins. His name was Charlie Hunter. He was an excellent shot, but he was not happy with his rifle. So he got Bert Riggall, who was an excellent gunsmith, to work it over by fitting it with a custom-built heavy target barrel thirty inches long and a long, sixteen-power Malcolm target telescope sight. He purchased a simple but effective outfit for reloading his ammunition. Then he practised till he knew exactly what his rifle could do. Any coyote that gave him a standing shot anywhere short of three hundred yards was money in his pocket. He could hit them on the run as well.

One morning I was out hunting along the foot of the mountains, when I spotted five coyotes about half a mile away as they rambled up an open slope across the Pincher Creek valley and over the rim of an open basin. I was about to start in pursuit when Charlie showed up riding his horse on their tracks. So I stayed to watch.

When he got up under the rim where the coyotes had disappeared, he tied his horse and sneaked up onto the skyline where he flattened out on his belly to look. It was only a short time before there came the sound of a shot followed by four more spaced out enough so he had plenty of time for accurate shooting. He came back to his horse, stepped up into the saddle, and rode over into the basin out of sight. I caught up to him in a patch of aspens in a big draw about half an hour later where he was busy skinning out four coyotes.

"Good shooting," I remarked.

"Should have had all five," he grumbled. "Missed the last one by two or three inches just before he got into a patch of brush."

Forty dollars was a fortune for a morning's hunting just the same. Charlie Hunter's ranch prospered, not from his cows, but from the fur he gathered from November to the end of January, when the quality of the pelts began to go down. He told me years later that after he got that rifle, he never borrowed another dollar from the bank. Charlie Hunter was well named, for he was a master hunter.

Poor as most of them were, prairie people rarely missed a chance to go to a picnic or any other kind of entertainment. A picnic was an opportunity to visit with neighbours, and it often included riding bucking horses, horse racing, foot racing, pitching horseshoes, and ball games. Sometimes some modest betting added a bit of spice to the contests. These affairs were a lot of fun. Men like Pat Burns sometimes put up a small cash prize for the winners of the cowboy contests and the cowboys themselves put some money into a hat to add to it, which naturally was a very popular move among the contestants. Small as the prizes were, they sparked a development that slowly grew.

I recall some of the ranchers and cowboys who organized a small rodeo in the country settlement of Twin Butte nearly sixty years ago. They pooled their resources, which were scanty enough, built a set of corrals, smoothed out an oval racetrack about half a mile long, and proceeded to advertise the event with newspaper announcements and posters. They gathered their own livestock for calf roping, and steer and bronc riding. People came for many miles driving their teams, and in cars and trucks. A couple of cowboys from a ranch fifty miles away hauled their roping horses with a homemade trailer hitched to an ancient truck, the first outfit of this kind that most of us had ever seen.

The day was clear and hot, and a crowd of three or four hundred had gathered to watch the events throughout the afternoon. By dusk, when they gathered at an open-air dance pavilion built in a grove of cottonwood close by Yarrow Creek, some ominous-looking clouds were gathering, and the dance had only been underway for about an hour when a storm cut loose with a barrage of thunder and a downpour of rain that sent everyone scrambling for their slickers and camps.

My brother and I had ridden about four miles to the show and in the impenetrable darkness we somehow managed to find our horses amid the many that were tied among the trees, without getting kicked by some of the half-broke broncs. We were soaked from head to foot when we hit the trail for home. We couldn't see our hands in front of our faces it was so dark, but had to depend on the horses to find the way. It was slow going. When we got within a mile of home, my horse, who was in the lead, walked over a bank on the edge of a new grade and fell about five or six feet down on to the road. Fortunately I came down on the high side of the wreck and never even got a bruise. We were two tired kids glad to shed our wet clothes and crawl into a dry bed that night.

It is doubtful if anyone made money at the show except perhaps for some of the contestants who had a few dollars in their pockets, but that was one of the first small rodeos that was held in that part of the country, the beginning of organ-ized annual rodeos generally held in town that have become part of a now accepted and well-supported business during the summer months.

In the old days the cowboys trained on the job. I remem-ber Herman Linder, who came to Alberta with his parents from Switzerland as a small boy, telling me how he and a brother fixed up a corral in the remote corner of the hills where they practised bronc riding on weekends, riding on horses that they had rounded up out of the many that roamed the range at that time. They even built a chute in which they saddled and got on the wild ones and then turned them loose into a corral.

Contest rules were flexible with regard to saddles then, and just about any saddle would do. Herman, like many of us, was riding a saddle that was too short in the seat to be a good bronc rigging. It was not until later that the international cowboys' association drew up the rules that dictated the stan-dard for a contest saddle. Such a rig must have no more than a fourteen-inch swell in the fork and a cantle not more than five inches high. The length of the seat was flexible, but most riders chose the sixteen-inch size. This became the so-called Association saddle, the recognized contest rigging. It was not till a friend loaned Herman such a saddle that he realized how much he had been penalizing himself with a short seat. Riding a rig that fit him perfectly he went on to win the North American saddle-bronc championship three times. Later he became a highly respected rodeo promoter and director, as well as a cattle rancher.

With Herman, ranching was a business but rodeo was his profession. He still lives part of the year on his ranch south-west of Cardston, Alberta. There is a collection of his trophy saddles and cowboy equipment in the Cowboy Hall of Fame in Oklahoma City, Oklahoma. Herman is now in his eighties but still active and he regularly attends the big shows as a spectator – a man who is a living legend.

While the first big rodeos were held in the larger western towns and cities – for example, the Calgary Stampede in Alberta and the Cheyenne Frontier Days in Cheyenne, Wyoming – near the turn of the century, uncounted smaller shows were held all over the west. There were also travelling shows, such as Colonel William Cody's Wild West Show, which toured the major cities of the midwest and eastern United States with Cody's extensive troupe of Indians and cowboys and various livestock, including buffalo. Cody was the first to tour Europe, where his show attracted big crowds, including various members of royalty.

Guy Weadick, promoter and manager of the first Calgary Stampede in 1912, failed to agree on a contract for a show the following year at that city, so he organized a series of rodeos across Canada, and also into Europe, where he and his cowboys and cowgirls were recognized by royalty.

As a boy, I remember seeing a team of Mexican *vaqueros* put on a dazzling display of roping as part of the Ringling Brothers circus in 1928 at Lethbridge, Alberta. One of the tricks was performed by a roper with a big open loop hung on the toe of his boot as he lay on his back. He threw the loop with his foot, catching five ridden horses by the front legs as they ran abreast past him. The whole show was put on in what they billed as "the biggest tent in the world" – the Big Top as they called it. These big circuses travelled by special trains in those days – trains put together specifically to transport the performers, work crew, animal trainers, animals, and various equipment. For two kids, fresh from a mountain ranch on the edge of wild country, and for their grandfather, it was all tremendously exciting and unforgettable.

Cowboy sport, as developed by the popularity of rodeo, has not only grown fast, but has been refined beyond those early contests born on the open range. The stock used are the best available, kept for no other purpose, and well looked after. While the early contestants were largely cowboys coming from a job on a ranch, the development of professional rodeo contestants has evolved from the catch-as-catch-can individuals recognized in cow country as top hands to highly trained athletes, many of whom never saw a bucking horse ridden or a calf roped and tied until they got to a college sponsoring a rodeo team among its various sports programs. There, interested and determined youngsters could train under professional coaches, attend special rodeo schools, and learn the game in a way a young ranch-raised cowboy would have never dreamed of being able to do fifty years ago.

The incentive most generally recognized is prize money. Among professional sports, rodeo is the poorest of them all. Contestants are not paid a salary. They do pay to register as a contestant in any show. They are protected to a certain extent by membership in their own association. For many their winnings are barely sufficient to live on, but for the best of them prize money can add up to many thousands over a given season. At the Calgary Stampede, the contestants compete for "day money" every day for ten days. The top purse for the finals is $50,000 per event.

Over the years the rodeo events have expanded to include saddle bronc riding, bareback bronc riding, calf roping, bulldogging, bull riding, chuckwagon racing, and barrel racing, as well as wild-horse racing and wild-cow milking. The riders are given fifty points for the ride and fifty for the horse or the bull. Every horse and bull has a name and the riders draw for their mounts. The ride lasts eight seconds, which may not seem like much, but believe me when I tell you that eight seconds on the top of the storm created by a grain-fed horse that may weigh up to sixteen hundred pounds, or by a brahma bull that can weigh up to a ton, can seem like a very long time.

Saddle bronc riding requires the rider to come out of the chute with his spurs set well forward on the horse's shoulders, and during the course of the ride the spurring must be forward and back every jump in unison and the same on both sides of the horse. The rider's right hand holds the soft, braided buck shank that is fastened to the halter on the horse's head, and his left hand swings high and free. If that hand touches either the horse or the saddle during the ride, the rider is disqualified. Saddle bronc riding is an exquisite combination of timing in balance with the horse's moves and the ability to take up the pounding that is the heart of the physical storm.

In bareback bronc riding, a surcingle – a leather pad with a grip for the rider's hand – is cinched around the horse, and that and the seat of his pants are his only contact with the horse. Here again an eight-second ride is the requirement. And again, the ride is scored equally between the rider and the horse. There is no way a rider can do anything but spur and lean back on the anchor of his hand. Bareback broncs are lighter, faster, and generally crooked with their action, so a cowboy not only has to depend totally on his hold on the handle of the surcingle but also on the fine timing of his balance.

Most of the rodeos fill in breaks in the program with a wild-horse race involving horses fresh off the range, where a three-man team of cowboys takes its mounts out of the chutes on the end of a rope. Apart from a saddle there is no other equipment. The contest is to stop the horse, get a close hold on its head and saddle it, then one man mounts and heads for a line drawn on the arena floor. It is much easier to talk about than do, for a wild horse can find many ways to cause a wreck in the midst of a whirling, plunging mix-up of a dozen or more animals trying to do the same thing to the teams of men trying to get them under some control. It's a first-class way to collect some painful rope burns, bruises, and even broken bones.

The wild-cow-milking contest involves teams of three men, one with a horse under him and the other two on foot, one with a pop bottle and a fair portion of optimism. The cows are turned out loose in the arena. The rider ropes a cow, takes his dallies on the saddlehorse and brings his catch to a stop; the second man grabs her by the head and holds her, whereupon the man with the bottle goes in close, grabs a teat, and proceeds to milk enough milk into the bottle to a depth of about an inch. Wild cows, being understandably very irate about this liberty and the intrusion on their privacy, may react with a well-aimed kick, which can cause complications that, along with much leaping and jumping, make life interesting for the cowboy with the bottle. Hitting the narrow neck of a bottle with a stream of milk can be difficult under such conditions. The man that gets the necessary amount of milk into the bottle and sprints to the spot where a judge is waiting wins the contest.

In the calf roping, the calf is put in a chute beside an open pen big enough to loosely hold the rider and his mount with a string barrier stretched across its open end. When the cowboy gets his mount properly positioned and ready the calf is turned loose, and when it crosses a line ten feet in front of the chute, the rider comes out, ropes it around the neck, stops it as he comes off his horse, grabs it and throws it, then ties three of its legs together with a short pigging string tucked in his belt with its open loop held in his teeth. A time less than eight or nine seconds usually places the contestant in the prize money. Breaking the barrier results in a ten-second penalty. It is a contest where the cooperation between a man and his horse is paramount, and the skill of throwing and tying the calf requires the utmost physical coordination on the part of the rider.

In the bulldogging contest, a steer, usually of the fast Mexican breed, weighing six or seven hundred pounds and wearing horns, takes the place of the calf in the chute with the wrestler on its left side and a hazer that keeps the animal running straight on its right. Again, the steer must cross a line before the barrier is broken. The wrestler runs his horse up alongside the animal at top speed, coming down with his arm over its neck to grasp its horns, stop it, and throw it flat on its side. Winning times can be as short as four seconds. Bulldoggers are usually big, tall men, as stopping and throwing a steer running at full speed takes plenty of muscle power.

Of all rodeo contests, bull riding is by far the most dangerous and spectacular. When a man comes out of the chute, on top of about a ton of Brahma bull bent on murder and mayhem, with one hand on a soft rope cinched tight around the bull's middle and the other swinging free, he knows he is up in a storm of muscle wrapped in loose hide. He's looking down at a wicked pair of horns and all that keeps him away from them is his grip on the rope and the rowels of his spurs digging into the bull's hide on its sides. If he and his balance stay on top of the bull, eight seconds can seem like an hour, and if he is thrown, his life may depend on the bullfighter out in front of the chute with the paint on his face and in a clown's baggy pants. Good bullfighters know how to pull a bull's attention from a fallen rider and how to hold it long enough for him to get away from the bull and up the nearest chute or fence. All rodeo cowboys live with danger to some degree, but bull riders know the difference between getting hit or missed can be measured in split seconds, and a good bullfighter's help can set up the missing edge in his favour. It's pretty wild, and purely wonderful how a bull rider can come out of a lethal mix-up with a whole skin. Getting thrown off a bull is one thing; dismounting after the signal horn goes, marking the end of eight seconds, can be just as dangerous, for there is nobody but the bullfighter to help when the rider hits the ground with a bull bent on wiping him out about two steps away.

At the other end of the spectrum is the cowgirls' barrel racing event where the young ladies race their highly trained mounts around three barrels set out in the arena. They go one at a time in this timed event, where a difference of a tenth of a second can put a rider in the prize money or out of it.

But at the end of the day, the chuckwagon race, a spectacle reminiscent of the old Roman chariot races, is a show unto itself. Four wagons, drawn by four fast horses, accompanied by four outriders, race around a set of barrels and out over an oval track. The starting gun sees the outriders load tent poles, a tent, and a stove into the wagon, then jump onto their horses as the chuckwagon driver weaves his running team in a figure 8 around a set of barrels. The trick is to do it without upsetting a barrel to avoid a time penalty. The four wagons hit the track at top speed, each in its own lane, the positions being drawn before the race. The horses are all thoroughbred racers. There are thirty-two of them running on the track at once, with outriders all running their mounts to get as close to their wagon as possible. Penalties are counted against any item being dropped in the loading of the wagons, against barrels being upset, and against a rider more than one hundred feet from his wagon at the finish line. The skill of the drivers reigning four running horses hitched to the wagons as they jockey for position around the track is phenomenal. To see the wagons coming against a red sunset, under a pall of dust down the home stretch, is something never to be forgotten. It is the classic spectacle of all rodeo sport. At the Calgary Stampede, sixteen to twenty wagons compete every evening – a fitting climax to a full afternoon of sustained action.

The cowboy was a physically tough breed, ready for anything adventurous, loyal to the brand for which he worked. He worked hard, went on the occasional binge, and played hard when the opportunity afforded. His character has changed some over the years, but he still loves the old-style action-and-adventure way of life.

I can remember when a cowboy yearning to compete in some rodeo would pack his bed on his top roping horse and lead it behind another horse maybe a hundred miles to the nearest railway station, where he would buy a ticket for himself and his mounts to take him to his destination. That might be New York's Madison Square Garden, Chicago, Denver, Calgary, some place in between, or even as far away as London, England, or Berlin, Germany, if he got on the payroll of a big show.

Now he puts his horse in a streamlined trailer pulled by a pickup truck and during the course of a busy season travels thousands of miles. Off-season he may run a rodeo school specializing in whatever type of competition he knows best through successful competition, or he may work with livestock on his home ranch.

Almost universally, successful rodeo contestants train to keep in top physical condition. They are outstanding athletes, for whatever type of rodeo contest is their specialty, they know that there is no other way to maintain that vital split-second timing necessary to get into the winning circle.

Among professional sports, rodeo is the poorest paid, expenses are high, and professional rodeo cowboys have to win to stay alive. Just the same, the indomitable determination that took them north on the big cattle drives travelling from Mexico to Canada, fording flooding rivers, fighting rustlers and hostile Indians along with everything the elements could throw at them, is still with them. Cowboy culture has changed to a degree, but the basic character of the man and his woman partner has not. They are the salt of the earth. Their kids grow up strong in the midst of historic tradition in which physical toughness and courage are the keynotes, and honesty, fairness, and a certain generosity of spirit are the highlights of their character.

CHAPTER 11

The Unknown Quantity

"Yuh cain't tell how far a frog kin jump by just lookin' at him," opined an old cowboy, and the history of those who ride with cows certainly proves it.

Cows sometimes have strange ways of expressing their gratitude when a man gets them out of a jam. This quirk of character was brought home to me one day when I was about thirteen or fourteen years old.

I was alone at the ranch, as everyone had gone to town. It was calving time, with about thirty head of very pregnant cows in the pasture near the buildings. Every two or three hours I would ride out to check them, and shortly after noon my patrol revealed a cow was missing. My search for her ended when I found her stuck in a lingering snowdrift in the bottom of a draw where the stream of run-off water had undermined it with a tunnel that came up close to the surface. The footing was too slippery for my horse to haul her

DON BRESTLER 93

out, so I went back to the barn, harnessed the work team, and hitched them to a set of double trees with a light logging chain attached.

When I drove down to the cow I slipped the chain around her horns and it didn't take very long to haul her out on to bare ground. Backing the team up to get some slack, I stepped to the cow to take the chain off her head, whereupon she jumped to her feet, let out a great roar, and charged. Pushing against the outside curve of one horn, I spun away from her to the side and she skidded by me to run into the team. They naturally spooked and headed for the barn on the run dragging the chain, which fortunately for her had come free of her head. Before I could do much more than blink my eyes, that miserable old blister of a cow swapped ends and came back at me with her tongue sticking out, and again I dodged. She ran past me out on to the snowdrift, broke through, and was just as solidly stuck as ever. I stood there and talked to her for a while and if my mother had heard me, she would have taken me by an ear and made me wash my mouth out with soap.

By the time I brought the team back and dragged her out a second time, she had apparently decided she was tired of snow, for she trotted off to go about the business of giving birth to a fine big calf. Sometimes cows are very indifferent about their social connections, if not about their own survival.

A couple of mornings later I was out at daylight checking the bunch when I found a newborn calf lying on its back in a hole near where its mother had dropped it. It seemed cold and nearly dead, so I picked it up, slid it across the fork of my saddle, then stepped up behind it to head for the barn, its mother coming along anxiously behind. The calf was hanging limply down both sides of my saddle with me keeping it balanced as my horse single-footed along, when all of a sudden it came to life, let out a bawl, and started to kick. My horse, which ordinarily would never think of bucking, bogged her head and cut loose, and about the second jump the calf went one way and I went the other, to come down flat on my back. When I sat up, it was to see the horse heading for the barn dragging the bridle reins to one side so she wouldn't step on them, and the calf was staggering off towards its mother. Sometimes it seems like a man just can't win.

Any kid growing up around cows at calving time gets an on-the-job education in the therapeutics of pregnancy and birth, much of which he may feel at the time would be wonderful to avoid.

When a calf comes normally, the front feet show first and then the head, and if it isn't too thick in the shoulders or hips, a few good strong heaves from its mother pushes it out. After that it won't be long before it is on its feet and looking for its first milk. But when things go wrong, like a front leg bent back, the only thing to do is push the calf back to give enough room to move the foot forward, and that is not easy when a cow is shoving hard against you. Working with an arm inside of a cow up to the shoulder is very difficult sometimes. When a calf comes backwards, it is a matter of pulling it out quickly before it smothers, and unless care is taken the little animal's back can be injured. We carried a pair of hobbles made of soft cotton rope to slip over a calf's feet to give us a better grip. More than once, I have used my lariat tied to my saddle-horn so the horse could help, a method that is entirely practical, but must be handled with care.

But there is a beautiful factor in all this which came to me a long time ago. The entire phenomenon of conception and birth is something of a wonderfully natural, yet mysterious process; the flowing and beginning of life. It is very delicate, yet there is a supreme physical toughness and strength involved that is salutary. If someone were to ask me what might be one of the most satisfying experiences of a long life, it would have to include helping a cow with a difficult birth, then watching her lick her baby dry and see it get to its feet and go stumbling towards a teat to get its first feed. I might be so damn glad to have it over that I am shaking, but I am satisfied to the core of my bones, and it doesn't matter much if it is a warm sunny spring morning or in the middle of a blizzard at night.

I remember trailing a heifer once in a spring snowstorm for a considerable distance and about dark finding her on the edge of a meadow surrounded by poplar and willow bush. Both front feet of the calf were showing but she was obviously in trouble. I threw my rope over her head and one front foot so she wouldn't choke down, then rode around a tree and pulled her up close to it. It was getting dark, so I gathered a pile of dead wood and lit a fire for some light. Then I went to work.

The heifer was a snorty, snaky two-year-old black Angus, at first not at all thrilled with me handling her, but she settled down after some preliminary fighting, seeming to know I wanted to help. With my sleeves rolled up as far as possible I felt inside of her to find that the calf's head was turned back, so I put the hobbles on its front feet and pushed it back as far as possible. It took some doing, but I managed to get its head straightened out. Then taking the lower jaw of the calf in one hand, the hobbles with the other, I pulled hard to get it started through the pelvic opening.

The cow flopped down on her side and I sat down behind her, braced my feet against her rump, and hauled. She was heaving too, and I timed my pulling with her muscle contractions so we were working together. In a few minutes the calf was out in the snow, all shiny and wet and very much alive. Slipping the rope off the heifer, I backed up to the fire and watched as she came up close to the calf, wide-eyed, and began to lick it dry. It wasn't very long till it was struggling to get up, and it sure knew where supper was. When it was full of milk, it lay down again, whereupon the heifer tossed her head at me a couple of times, warning me she would have no more nonsense with her new daughter, so I got on my horse and went home feeling fine. It was a good sheltered place and she and her calf would come back when they were ready.

Contrary to popular belief, there is not much romance but a lot of hard work connected with being a cowboy. Just the same, for a youngster who doesn't mind the work, there is allure in the dress, association with horses and cows, and skill that is spiced with a certain wildness. Sometimes riding out there with the sun chinning itself on the eastern horizon in the early morning and the feel of a good horse under me, I felt so chock-full of high spirits that I couldn't help giving a wild yell that echoed off the hills.

I couldn't afford any fancy rigging, but what I had got the work done. Just the same, like every other kid in cow country, I collected saddle catalogues and dreamed about a hand-tooled rigging with fancy chaps, spurs, and boots. Some of the cowboys I knew had angora woolskin chaps; their bridle bits and spurs were adorned with silver inlays, and their boots had sixteen- and seventeen-inch tops all stitched with silk. My father wore black angora woolskin chaps of shotgun style and a pair of made-to-order boots, but he never went much for silver on his bridle bit. He never wore spurs, claiming a horse that was properly trained didn't need them. Occasionally on some horses he hung a braided quirt on his saddle, but he rarely used it. He was a great rider who rode a horse like he was part of it, and he was a really fine roper.

When we branded the calves in the spring, the neighbours came to help. It was a kind of social event on every ranch, when we traded work. Dad was always in demand with his horse and rope, for without hurrying he could keep two wrestling teams busy. Each calf was roped by the heels and dragged to the fire, where the wrestlers threw it down and took off the rope, one man taking the hind feet and the other the front to hold the calf to be dehorned, vaccinated, castrated (if it was a bull), and branded. The whole process only took two or three minutes on average. The kid of the crew usually tended the fire and passed hot irons, which kept him on the jump if he did it right. A good crew of a dozen men could put two hundred calves through the process in a short afternoon.

I remember helping at a branding at a ranch on the edge of the Blood Indian Reserve one time; a day in June with the temperature at about ninety degrees. We branded about one hundred and fifty calves and twenty colts in four of the hottest, dustiest, thirstiest hours I ever spent. I was about fifteen. The water supply was cold and clear, a spring with enough alkali in it to be undrinkable to anyone not accustomed to it. To a mountain boy used to pure water, that stuff could induce a two-day session of the Rocky Mountain two-step that was the next thing to cholera, so I went thirsty. By noon my mouth felt like it was lined with flannel, when the boss showed up with a wooden beer keg nested in a tub full of ice. He handed me a mug full of the foaming cold stuff, which tasted like something from heaven. By the time I was well into my second mug, I was sitting in the shade of the corral with my back to a post, feeling no pain, with an inclination to sing but scared to start. That was my first taste of an alcoholic beverage, but strangely enough, I have never really enjoyed beer since unless I was hot and thirsty.

My father would take a drink on occasion, but never more than one. As for my mother, she was an adamant temperance woman, who strongly recommended her sons to be teetotallers. Few of the cowboys I really admired drank heavily, if at all, but some went on occasional binges that could last for days.

There was one aspect of mother's rigid opposition to drinking that I look back at with some amusement. Every spring she would gather dandelion blooms and proceed to make a couple of gallons of wine in a stone crock, which was put away in a cold corner of the basement. When March rolled around the following year, she would pour us all a tumbler full of this brew, which had a tangy, not unpleasant flavour, and we drank it. Spring tonic, she said, and I guess it was, but on occasion it was high enough in alcohol to make getting to bed upstairs something that required concentration. She seemed oblivious to the fact that we all got pretty jolly.

My brother John and I were constantly on the move, working with horses and cattle, fishing, hunting, and trapping when we weren't in school. We were very active and gloried in the freedom of wild country. When we got old enough to take in the schoolhouse dances round the country, some of the young bucks would sometimes have a bottle with them. There would be the occasional fight, which proved nothing very much, because too much drink was the usual cause. John and I both enjoyed dancing; the drinking cut down the competition for partners and we took advantage of it. Rides that could add up to thirty miles, round trip, to get to a dance added up to a lot of exercise, and we sometimes didn't get home till the sun was up.

When the temperatures were well below zero with a north wind adding to the chill riding anywhere was an exercise in endurance. One of us would always ride the fourteen miles to town on Christmas Eve to get the mail and whatever odds and ends of groceries that mother wanted. I made one ride when it was twenty-odd degrees below zero straight into the teeth of a nasty north wind. It was so cold that I had to get off my horse and walk ahead of him – not easy with all the clothes I had on plus Dad's woolskin chaps. My saddle, like most of them, had a hole under its fork below the horn and, chaps designed as they are, the wind whistled through, chilling my crotch. I finally got so numb with cold that I stopped at a ranch belonging to a French Canadian to warm up. He had a numerous family, including a daughter about my age, and when I came in the door the good lady of the house, surrounded by kids, was all smiles as she helped me off with my coat. About that time the daughter put a big mug of hot cocoa on the kitchen table which I gratefully sipped while feeling the warmth spread out all through me. Suddenly I became aware of thawing out, for a painful burning sensation assailed me in a very private part of my anatomy. It was pure agony and I stood up from the table to stamp around in a sort of wild dance with my face tied in a knot.

"Must be chilblains," I gasped. "It'll be all right in a minute."

As soon as possible I escaped through the door, thanking the lady, and, wishing them all a Merry Christmas, got back on my horse and headed for town.

After I had tied my horse in a stall at the livery stable, I sneaked a look at my still throbbing appendage. It was so tender I could scarcely stand to touch it. As I looked after my errands, I worried it would drop off like calves' tails sometimes did when they froze. The trip back home was made in record time and was much warmer with the wind in my back. For a few days I was very careful when moving around, but kept my misfortune to myself. Urinating was very painful for a while. In due course I healed up, but knowing I would be very sensitive to cold I made some preparations for another hard day in the saddle, should it come.

Through some talk or reading I had done, I knew the old Indians protected themselves on cold rides by making a sheath from a weasel skin and tying it with a cord around their waists. So I picked a suitable skin out of the collection taken on my trapline and proceeded to tan it. For the rest of the winter I wore it with the fur in against my skin all the time. Come spring I hung it up in the back of my clothes closet, where my mother found it while cleaning house.

"What on earth is this?" she asked me.

So I told her and she handed it back to me as she shook her head and left looking somewhat amazed. When my father heard about it, he roared with laughter. He also told me that some of the old cowboys had used such a contraption in winter.

Another time on a winter ride to town, a cold blizzard blew in mid-afternoon. The snow driving on the wind made the ride home a long one. Visibility was down to a few yards in a white-out as it got dark and it was hard to see the trail. It was some better by the time I got into the hills a few miles from home, when I caught sight of another rider ahead of me. I had stepped my horse into a trot to catch up to him when I saw him topple out of his saddle into the snow. His horse stopped, and I got down to find a young halfbreed by the name of Joe Lawrence whom I had gone to school with lying peacefully asleep and drunk as a lord. With no little difficulty I finally got him back to life and on his horse. He had a burlap sack with a gallon jug of cheap wine tied into both ends and slung across the front of his saddle, and a bottle of brandy in each of his overcoat pockets. He had been working on one of these bottles, "to keep from freezing" he told me. He was bringing his contribution to a "forty-gallon dance" his father was going to host in celebration of somebody's birthday. He would never have reached it, if I hadn't happened to come along that night, for he would have frozen solid before morning. As it was, he was singing when I left him at his father's door.

Nobody really knows how deep his personal power of endurance runs until he tries it out, and even then the real depth may not be reached. On a mountain ranch like the one I grew up on working with my father, I found out about some personal limitations when still not fully grown.

Hauling hay for the cattle was a daily chore. Dad would hitch the team up to a bobsleigh in the morning, drive to a stack, and fill the eight-by-sixteen-foot basket rack with loose hay, then take it to the cattle and throw it off in a long line until they had about twenty to twenty-five pounds apiece. In normal weather it was just work that had to be done, not taking very much effort, but when a blizzard blew in with the cold running far below zero it was something else. Not only did it take more hay but working in the cold took a lot more energy.

It was mid-January one winter when a blizzard blew in dropping two feet of snow. Then it cleared and the temperature went down to forty below zero. My father came down with flu and was flat on his back in bed with fever and hurting all over. So it was up to me to see that the cattle were fed. I was about thirteen years old.

Up well before daylight, I threw hay and oats into the manger in front of our big team, and then wrestled the heavy harness on them. Leaving them to feed I went back to the house where Mother had a hot breakfast ready. Then I hitched up the team to the sleigh and drove to a stack on the other side of the ranch, picking up an old cowboy on the way who lived in a log cabin with his wife and daughter. Phil Lucas was a tough, stringy old Irishman with a crippled hand. Together we forked the loose hay on to the rack and spread it for the cattle, while sun-dogs glittered in a steely sky. Then we loaded the rack again.

That work filled the morning. After lunch we fed the cattle that were kept close to the buildings, then I took Phil home. By the time the team was watered, fed, and put in the barn for the night, the wood box filled and other chores done, the stars were out. At night I did more than sleep, I passed out. It seemed as though I had just closed my eyes when the alarm clock cut loose. Sometimes I slept through its clamour and then Mother would come and shake me awake.

The days were just a blur of unending cold, tired muscles, creaking hoofs and sleigh runners, and the steamy smell of horses. One night the thermometer dropped to fifty-two below, but it didn't seem that much colder when I went out the next morning.

On the way to the haystack old Phil told me, "Your nose is froze. Gotter thaw it out with your hand." I took a look at him to see his beaky wind-splitter was frozen white as a bone. "Yours is froze solid," I told him. He felt it gingerly and cussed, "Damn if it ain't! Hard enough to peck holes in a board!"

I couldn't help laughing and he looked hard at me past the hand that was holding his nose in a way that shut me up. Then he chuckled and remarked, "We can still laugh anyways. Things could be worse."

Later that morning I think Phil might have wondered. We had thrown about half the load off and Phil was standing at the back of the rack, when I moved the team ahead. They were slow to move and I popped one with the end of my lines over the rump and yelled at them. They jerked the sleigh into motion, whereupon Phil went over the end of the rack backwards. On the way the back of his overalls caught on one of the pegs where the ends of the willow staves stuck up through the two-by-four forming the end of the basket and pulled his pants down around his knees. He lit on his rump in the snow with the end gate of his longjohns unbuttoned. When he got up, the air was blue with his swearing as he got his clothes back where they belonged. He was still swearing when he climbed back up on to the load. I wanted to laugh so bad I could hardly breathe, but this time I managed somehow to keep a straight face. Phil finally ran out of breath or bad words, I don't know which, but I can still recall his look of unbridled outrage.

If I had aspirations to become a cowboy, this part I could do without. There seemed to be no end to the cold. Dad was up and moving around again but too weak to do very much. I couldn't remember how it felt not to be tired.

Then one evening just as we were finishing supper, the house suddenly cracked. Dad went to the door and looked out. "It's a chinook!" he exclaimed. "It feels warm as summer!"

Next morning it was forty above with water dripping from the eaves of the house. The temperature had risen about ninety degrees in fourteen hours. In three days the hills were bare on the south slopes and the stock was lazing around enjoying the warmth. The wind continued to blow soft and warm, and apart from a few short snowstorms the back of the winter had been broken.

Hard weather in winter is one thing, but when snow and cold holds on stubbornly into spring, the life of a cowman can be tough. In the old days on the open range, cows were pretty much left to themselves and very much alone when calving. It was a stark matter of survival of the fittest. If a cow was prone to calving trouble, she usually died before she was very old, so genetics arranged it so they rarely had trouble compared to the pampered cattle we know today. Veterinarians were few and far between and such things as antibiotic injections and caesarian operations were unknown. It is amazing what a healthy cow can stand and even more impressive what newborn calves can survive, though there was a preponderance of bobbed tails and cropped ears among them from being frozen in a bad spring.

After I began to work away from home, my life was tied up mostly with horses. Range mares rarely have any trouble with a birth – I can't remember ever helping one. I may have lost one or two due to birthing problems but never found anything but bones picked clean by scavengers.

Not long ago, I recall reading an article on how to train a young horse to go into water and realized this could be a problem with horses kept close to a barn. It was no problem with range horses, especially those raised along rivers. They learned to swim as young sucking colts. Many's the time I have seen mares in swimming water with their colts, snuggled up against their upstream flanks, striking out strongly with no fear. Some horses raised where the streams are small never learn to swim, but they are few and far between. I have encountered only two or three in my life. It can be an embarrassing thing to find out when you have taken a horse into swimming water.

One time my brother John and I were out looking for some of our horses that had strayed away from the bunch we were using in my outfitting business at Waterton Park. He finally found them grazing on a meadow out amongst a mess of beaver dams along the Waterton River. How they got there was a mystery, for the place was a maze of water, big trees, and brush. We were sitting our saddles wondering how to get to them with a deep, clear beaver pond in front of us under a low, fairly steep bank.

"They'll know how they got there," John said. "I'll swim my horse across and get behind them."

So saying, he jumped his horse, Peanuts, into six feet of water. Peanuts went clear to the bottom, kicked up a cloud of silt, came up and grabbed a big breath, then promptly went to the bottom again. Thus he crossed the pond leaving a string of silt clouds in his wake.

When John rode him out on the far side, I yelled, "For God's sake! You know enough to loosen your cinch before heading into deep water!"

"My cinch is loose," John came back. "This horse can't swim!"

I didn't believe it. But that night we pushed Peanuts into a deep hole on Pass Creek, as we took the saddlehorse bunch out to pasture. He crossed the swimming water in exactly the same way, going in great bounds.

It was not long after this that John and one of my top wranglers, Bob Thomas, got into a mix-up in swimming water that could have been the end of both of them.

East of the village of Waterton and directly under the Prince of Wales Hotel is the Narrows, a neck between the Upper and Lower Waterton lakes. We used to cross there with our horses when we took parties up to Crypt Lake. The people were taken by launch up to Hell Roaring Canyon Landing, where we picked them up. We would take the horses in a long string, each one tied to the tail of the horse ahead, with a mounted wrangler in the lead and another bringing up the rear. Slim Udel ran a boat-rental service at the docks up by the village, so we would arrange to have him meet us at the crossing, where he would lead the whole string across the swimming water on the end of a long rope. I had made a long standing order that my wranglers were never to try to cross without a boat, for it was a treacherous place; the water was icy cold most of the summer, and at high water time, it was just too risky.

One fine morning in early July, John and Bob took about a dozen horses up to the crossing. For some reason or other Slim was not there to meet them. So they decided to swim the bunch across. Bob was in the lead on a good horse, with John trailing on a half-broke bronc we called Chubbins. About halfway across in eighteen feet of water the string caught up to Bob and the next thing he knew there were horses milling all around him. Fortunately he had taken off his boots and chaps, so he was able to leave his horse and dive under the circle of horses and begin swimming back. But the lead horse of the string spotted him and the next thing he knew he was again in the middle of a mill with horses all around him. He was a powerful swimmer and again he dove under them.

In the meantime John's horse decided that she wanted to go back to the corrals, which were located about six hundred yards east across a big bay. He splashed water on her face from the side trying to turn her, but she laid her ears back flat and kept right on going. So he put the loop of his lariat over her head and proceeded to choke her, knowing she would have to stop and would float up enough to make him a raft to hold on to until help arrived. When she turned halfway around with her nose pointed to shore, and showed signs of wanting to go there, he loosened the rope and she started swimming again with him trailing behind holding on to her tail.

In the meantime Slim Udel had arrived with his boat to help Bob, who was lying on the shore absolutely beat, retching up water he had swallowed, and the string of horses had come back to the beach.

I saw the water flying at the Narrows from my car on the

highway and drove up onto the hill by the hotel in time to see John come out with his horse on the far side and the rest of the string hit the beach on the near side. It was about as scary an experience for all concerned as we ever ran into over many years of guiding and outfitting, but all the horses and both men got safely to shore, though Bob's new boots and spurs rested somewhere down on the bottom of the lake. A couple of days later, he and John took a boat and went looking for them. They spotted the shining new spurs and Bob dove in to retrieve them. All three of us are getting long in the tooth now, but none of us has forgotten that adventure.

All it takes is a moment of bad judgement or the flickering finger of fate to be in the midst of a life-threatening situation. In this instance we all knew that we had been very lucky indeed.

CHAPTER 12

Some Hazards
of the Game

In the early days of ranching on an open range, when thousands of cattle were running free, there was no way for a foreman and his crew of cowboys to keep constant contact with the cattle wearing their ranch's brand. But they kept their cattle on their chosen range as much as possible, at the same time watching for rustlers and four-legged predators, as well as keeping an eye on any bogs dangerous to cows. These were common problems and there was cooperation practised in controlling them, just as there is today.

The cattle had taken the buffalo's range, but they acquired some of the predatory features of nature along with the territory. The Indians, accustomed to bounteous living off of buffalo, acquired a taste for beef, thus giving the ranchers cause for considerable concern. Some ranchers hated them for their depredations; others accepted the losses as part of living

DON BRESTLER 93

in this big country. The Mounted Police did a salutary job of keeping the peace.

Occasionally a homesteader, with his sod shanty filled with hungry children, killed a beef, but it was organized rustling that hurt the ranchers most and posed a real problem for the police. While their horseback patrols covered an enormous area, they were few in number, and the background of most of them in the force did not include the kind of experience necessary to deal with these thieves. But in spite of their many other duties, they tried hard to cope with organized rustling rings. Special stock detectives, plainclothes men familiar with the range and cattle business, were sometimes employed. But there weren't many of them and quite often they were a long way away when someone needed them.

I cannot give his real name, so I will call him Jim. He had been raised on a cow ranch. Being a recent graduate of the Police Academy, his experience as an officer was short, but his experience with horses and cattle was much longer, so when he was assigned a big area of southeastern Alberta just north of the international boundary, he was on familiar ground.

In between routine duties, Jim rode far and wide across the prairies and through the hills trying to gather concrete evidence of rustling, which he was sure was being practised by several ranchers working in an organized group on both sides of the border. Outwardly they appeared to be leading exemplary lives, but from bits and scraps of information, Jim was convinced of some mighty fishy activity, although he had nothing solid to pin on anybody. Reports of missing livestock kept coming in from various sources and his superior officer was getting more and more restive.

One day as Jim was riding past a set of corrals at a little

prairie loading station along the railway he noticed something. The corrals were being used as a sort of community branding facility and the brands of most of the ranchers in that part of the district were neatly hung on nails along the top rail of the main pen near the gate. The sight of the irons gave him an idea. It was highly unethical – even illegal – but Jim had a wild hair or two of his own, and the mischievousness of it appealed to him. He knew if he was ever found out, he would be in big trouble. He would need some luck.

A rodeo was being held in a few days at Medicine Hat, so he waited, knowing that just about everybody would be away enjoying this celebration. At dawn one morning he was out on his best horse scouting the country around the pens before beginning to round up all the loose horses he could find in the vicinity. By mid-morning he had quite a bunch in the corrals, and was pleased to note that the spring colts were all unbranded.

He built a fire out of scrap wood around the corrals, heated the irons required, and went to work. Had he not been a strong man and an excellent roper, the job would have been impossible. He used up most of the day roping colts, throwing them, tying them down, and branding them. He used one suspect's brand on horses belonging to another. He even exercised some considerable art in altering brands on some of the colt's mothers. In short, he raised some particular kind of hell, all the while keeping a wary eye open for approaching riders. Finally he hung up the irons and tidied up the corrals a bit and turned the horses loose. Then he headed out for home.

When the ranchers discovered the switched and altered brands, there was a terrific uproar. Somebody had been playing mighty bold with their horses. But who? Nobody even suspected a Mounted Police officer would do such a thing.

There was a lot of narrow-eyed suspicious talk as Jim went around doing his duty trying to track down the careless customer who had wielded the irons. Needless to say, it remained one of the unsolved cases on the police files. None of the suspects ever quite trusted the others again and the rustling stopped. They all knew that somebody was aware of what had been going on, and with the finger of suspicion pointing in all directions, it was a wise conclusion.

This was a fine example of fighting fire with fire. It saved the taxpayers a lot of money and was very effective. Twenty years later Jim was still laughing about it. "For a bunch so fast and loose about what they did with other people's stock, they were some fussy!" he opined, as he wound up the story.

The first stock detective hired by the Mounted Police was Jack Reid, who has been previously mentioned in this book. Son of Bill Reid, Jack was born and raised on a ranch located on the Little Missouri River in North Dakota upstream from the big ranch owned by Teddy Roosevelt and the town of Medora close to the Montana–North Dakota border.

He came to Canada in 1913 and worked as foreman looking after a herd of steers for Pat Burns. Rustlers were operating in the area and in due course they killed three steers in Jack's care. He did some riding and looking, which led him to suspect two brothers, hard-scrabble types living on a small ranch downriver from the Burns holding. Not far from their place, he found the hides from the butchered steers, with the brands cut out, hidden in some brush growing in a draw. A short distance away, he found the heads of the three butchered cattle in the bottom of a deep washout.

One of the steers was a "marker," brindle with some distinctive white spots. Its hide could be admissible evidence on the testimony of several men who knew it, but Jack was fully aware that such evidence is always shaky in court without the brands, so he proceeded to watch the brothers until one day they left the ranch in a wagon heading for Calgary.

Accompanied by one of his riders, Jack rode to their buildings to have a look around. Without a police officer or a search warrant such a manoeuvre had definite limitations, and as he sat his horse in the middle of the yard asking himself where the suspects would likely hide three pieces of hide with the damning brands, his eyes came to rest on their outhouse. Dismounting, he walked over and entered it and a minute later he called his rider.

When the cowboy came to the door of the john there was Jack with a lighted match in his hand peering down the hole in the scat, and he called attention to the fact that the waste below looked like it had been recently disturbed. It didn't take them long to find a shovel, upset the outhouse, and begin digging. Sure enough this brought the three patches of missing hide to light and some application of water revealed the Burns brand on all of them.

Charges were laid and in due course the brothers were arraigned in court. There, as the chief witness for the Burns ranch, Jack presented his evidence in great detail by arranging the bits of hides and heads together like jigsaw-puzzle pieces right there on the floor of the courtroom in front of the judge – a very odious business in a heated room full of people. Everyone, including the prisoners, was likely very happy when it was over. The rustlers confessed their guilt and were sentenced to a stretch in the penitentiary.

The Mounted Police were so impressed that they offered Jack a job as a stock detective in the force with the rank of sergeant and no further training necessary – probably the only time in their history that they made such a move. He accepted and was instrumental in breaking up several organized rustling rings.

Ranchers of the Maple Creek region of Saskatchewan were suffering mysterious losses of cattle and every effort to find the thieves had been fruitless, so Jack was sent to work on it. He was supplied with the money to lease a small ranch and stock it with cattle. As usual, he wore no uniform and realistically posed as a cowman starting up his own cow operation. He worked hard, got acquainted with his neighbours, listened to talk, and watched with unending patience.

Months went by and in due course suspicion centred on a rancher named Schultz, who not only owned some land and cattle but also a butcher shop in town. Jack made his acquaintance and found him a dour, taciturn man not given to being very friendly with anyone. But they had one thing in common, a love for good guns, which opened the door to better relations between them. Jack found that Schultz carried a fine German Luger semi-automatic pistol in a shoulder holster. He also learned that Schultz had formerly ranched near Shelby, Montana.

On the pretext of buying some more cattle, Jack went to Montana to do some backtrailing. Inquiry uncovered some interesting information about Schultz that pointed to rustling and murder, though nobody had been able to pin it on him. It also revealed that he had hired a young cowboy, who was very well liked, and who had been dragged to death by his horse at the end of his rope tied hard and fast to his saddle-horn. What had aroused suspicion about this supposedly accidental death was the fact that the victim was well known as a fine roper who never tied his rope. Perhaps the cowboy had discovered that he was working for a thief and quarrelled with his boss, and then been knocked down and tied to his horse. Whatever happened, the feelings of various people had run high and Schultz had disappeared. Jack did some careful searching and located some of the cowboy's relatives, one of whom supplied him with a small photo of the unfortunate young man, and there his search ended.

Returning to Saskatchewan, Jack bided his time for several months. One early-fall night under a full moon two riders showed up to cut out several of his big steers, which they drove away. Keeping out of sight, Jack trailed them for several hours, until they eventually drove the cattle into the pen at the back of Schultz's butcher shop. There he arrested the butcher and two cowboys in the act of butchering one of the steers. They were a tough, close-mouthed trio and refused to answer any questions, so Jack left them in the custody of the Mounted Police and headed for Schultz's ranch, arriving there about breakfast-time in his car.

When Schultz came out of his cabin to greet him, Jack knew he was armed. Jack was also wearing his Colt .44-40 six-shooter in a shoulder holster under his jacket. Alert and wary, he carefully reached into his shirt pocket, and without saying a word he handed Schultz the photograph of the cowboy he was suspected of killing.

Schultz took one look at it, turned pale, and stiffened as though about to reach for his gun. Jack had him pinned with the coldest grey eyes imaginable and his hand was poised within inches of his gun as he said, "You are under arrest for stealing cattle." Schultz remained frozen for a moment longer, then wilted. He was disarmed and handcuffed and taken to town to join his crew in jail.

The rustlers were all sentenced to two years in the penitentiary. When Schultz was finally released, he was only a shell of his former self. He holed up in an old cabin in the Cypress Hills, where he was found dead a few months later.

When Jack told me the story, he remarked that Schultz had undoubtedly lived in constant fear of arrest for murder and the worry contributed to his death – a kind of indirect justice.

Though we were of two generations, Jack Reid and I were great friends for many years. He eventually gave me the Colt .44-40 six-shooter he had carried for such a long time as a stock detective, police officer, and cowboy. It has been a reminder of a real frontiersman now gone over the great divide.

There were and still are four-legged predators that prey on ranchers' cattle. When the buffalo were wiped out, the prairie lobo wolves naturally went after beef, and their depredations were something to keep a rancher awake at night. The cattlemen hired wolfers, ironically many of them men who had hunted down buffalo, and paid bounty on the wolf scalps. Some ranchers kept packs of big, specially trained hounds to run them down. Teddy Roosevelt told of such hunts in which he took part in North Dakota when he was a young man. Thousands of wolves were poisoned with strychnine planted in the carcasses of cows and horses and many were trapped and shot. Jack Reid told me that when he was a teenager, he had on several occasions crawled into occupied wolf dens with a flare made from a coal-oil-soaked rag bound to a stick in one hand and his six-shooter in the other. A bitch wolf will not fight in her den, but the concussion of a .45 or .44 Colt pistol must have been horrendous in the cramped space and likely contributed to his later deafness.

At times the cowboys pursued wolves on horseback and roped them. My father told me of such an incident, when he and another cowboy jumped two big wolves off a cow they had just killed near the Little Bow River southeast of Calgary. Both wolves were stuffed with beef and consequently slow, so they had no trouble roping one, which they killed. But meanwhile the other wolf regurgitated its bellyful of meat, and when they rode in pursuit of it they were left far behind in the rough country alongside the valley.

Any time cowboys found a wolf den with pups in it they dug them out and destroyed them. George Lane of the Bar U Ranch and some of his crew jumped a family of wolves close to their den one day not far from High River. The parents fled but the half-grown pups dove into the den. The cowboys were in something of a dilemma, for they had no shovel. But then they spotted a freight train coming along the track a half a mile away. George rode out and flagged it down and borrowed a shovel from the fireman, and they proceeded to dig out the den while the train waited. Freight trains were obviously in not much of a hurry in those days.

Thus the wolves were largely wiped out in ranching country, but some of them survived in the foothills and mountains. Even today, a pack occasionally shows up in ranching country in Alberta and British Columbia.

Grizzly bears once roamed the prairies as far east as Lake Winnipeg and the Mississippi River. They were, as today, largely vegetarian, but also fed on buffalo – to a large extent crippled ones and those killed by wolves. When the buffalo disappeared, the hide hunters turned to hunting the big bears for their skins. There is a record of fifteen hundred grizzly pelts being taken in 1874 by one trader just east of the Cypress Hills on the Alberta-Saskatchewan border. Thus harried, a few surviving prairie grizzlies holed up in the foothills and mountains of southwestern Alberta, where a few of them learned to prey on cattle, and a few cattle are still killed by them.

The grizzlies' love of carrion moves the big animal to clean up any carcass found on its range and also causes them to be blamed for killing many animals dead from accident or disease. Many ranchers developed a kind of paranoia about bears in general, and as a result killed them at every opportunity. But the fact remains: few of them ever learn to kill cattle.

But predators of two legs or four received the blunt end of

heavy attack anywhere in cow country. During the 1880s in Wyoming and Montana, when the rough element of cowboy culture became too overbearing, vigilante committees were set up to hunt down and hang rustlers. As always in this kind of action, justice was final but not always right. Innocent men sometimes lost their lives at the end of a rope. Others not so innocent saddled up a fast horse and, riding mostly at night, made their way north across the border into Canada. There they came under the protection of the Mounted Police and, unless there was sufficient evidence to extradite them, they stayed in Canada – some of them to settle down as solid law-abiding citizens.

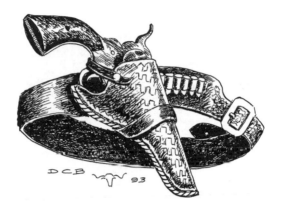

CHAPTER 13

George and Frenchy

DON BRESTLER 93

One of the characters that I remember with a good deal of nostalgia is George Gladstone, a Scotch-Cree halfbreed whose father was involved with the building of a number of the Hudson's Bay Company's trading posts across the vast country between Manitoba and points to the north and west. He was an expert log man with great skill in the use of an axe, adze, and crosscut saw. George was one of a numerous family, a tall wiry horseman who could handle just about any kind of job, from guiding and cowpunching to breaking horses, trapping, and entertaining a bunch of dudes around a campfire. Youngsters came to him like bees to honey. Let George show up and kids just naturally gravitated his way, for he loved them and they were fascinated with him. While George would go to any length to entertain and instruct a child, he would go just as far or even farther to play a joke on

one of his peers. You might get really angry at his pranks but you couldn't stay that way very long.

When I was a very young and ambitious trapper gathering spending money by trapping weasels, mink, and muskrats, I recall telling George about failing to catch a mink that dodged my trap and stole the bait. He told me to get a trap and show him how I set it, which I proceeded to do by building a little pen with three walls and a roof out of scraps of wood. The bait went into the back of it and the trap into the open front, so that an animal trying to get the bait would step into the trap.

When it was ready, George took the role of the mink, his hand pantomiming its actions as it circled the pen. It darted into a gap in my cubby, as we called the pen, and deftly stole the bait, whereupon it celebrated by leaping and jumping all over the place. I fixed the cubby. Again George's hand came back skipping around, then slipped in another hole and again stole the bait.

Then George built a cubby out of some rocks that were handy – a very solid little pen. He placed the bait in the back of it and artfully hid the trap itself under some dry grass.

Once more George's hand mimicked the actions of a questing, hungry mink as it examined the pen. There was no way in except from the open front and suddenly the trap snapped on his fingers, whereupon he went over backwards with a screech as he thrashed around with the trap hanging from his hand. I was reduced to a helpless heap convulsed with laughter at his clowning.

I remember him watching a neighbour breaking a big colt to ride and there was some question as to who was the most clumsy, but the colt won the contest by bucking the would-be bronc rider off on his head. George let out a great roar of laughter, which made the man angry.

"Let's see you ride him," he said.

"Hell," George came back, "I'll ride him backwards."

In one leap he was in the saddle facing the horse's tail and rode the horse as it bucked across the corral. When it tried to turn at the rail fence, it got its feet crossed and fell down, whereupon George grabbed it by the head and made a big show of being very concerned about its wellbeing as he held it down and talked to it. I don't know whether the horse or its owner learned anything from the process, but the rest of us were doubled up with helpless laughter. There was nothing George loved more than making people laugh and he rarely missed a chance.

He was out in the mountains guiding a pair of young hunters from Minneapolis, Minnesota, one fall, when they spotted a fine silvertip grizzly with its rump showing out of a big hole it had dug in pursuit of a marmot. It was far out of rifle range, so George led his hunters on a circuitous route over a considerable stretch of very rough country to a spot on top of a ridge about a hundred and fifty yards up the slope from the bear. There still wasn't much to see of the bear, which had most of its body hidden in the hole and George watched it through his binoculars while his hunters readied themselves to shoot. After several minutes, George whispered, "That bear is asleep. I'll go wake him up."

To the utter horror of his two neophyte companions, he walked casually down the slope and kicked the bear soundly in the rump. It was dead.

George could piece together what had happened. The bear had dug down after the marmot, which was out of reach under a big rock. The bear had tugged, dug, and doubtless sworn in grizzly language as it tried to get at the animal. It finally got its paws locked under the edges of the rock and heaved, while the marmot trembled and chirped with fright. But the rock didn't move. Whether the bear couldn't get his paws free, or whether it was the victim of a ruptured blood vessel, George was unable to say, but when he and his hunters finally managed to free it, the bottom of the hole was full of blood.

George had spotted the bluebottle flies on the bear through his glasses from the top of the ridge, and he couldn't resist the chance to play a joke on his hunters.

Periodically George worked for Harold Butcher, who had a ranch up the Drywood above our ranch, close to where a stream came out of the mountains. George was something of an eccentric and so was Butcher and each was always waiting for a chance to play a joke on the other.

I remember George telling me about a time when he and his boss were riding fence lines along a trail up a steep slope through a thick grove of lodge pole pines. George was riding in the lead when a slim dead pole that was lying on a slant almost parallel to the trail got hung up in Butcher's chap leg. His horse kept going and the pole upended till Butcher was hanging almost upside-down with his feet higher than his head. George stopped his horse, caught Butcher's horse by the bridle, and backed it up. But just as his horse was about free, he pretended the horses were getting out of hand and they went forward again till Butcher was once again hanging upside-down. It was a pantomime of repetition until Butcher's cursing moved George to end it with solicitous concern for his welfare which was so artfully acted that George almost believed it himself.

When he was about fifty George got a blood infection from bad teeth and became very ill. He knew he was going to die and told his cowboy friends that he wanted no weeping over him at his funeral. "Go to town," he told them, "and have a big party!"

This they did. It was a big and memorable funeral for a man who loved to make people laugh – and as far as anybody knew one who never did a really mean thing to anybody in his life.

George's sister, Nellie, was married to a big Frenchman, Henry Rivière, who went by the name of Frenchy. Frenchy was six-feet-four, with the longest legs I ever saw on a man. When he sat down he looked of average height, but when he stood up, he towered. He was born in France, the youngest son of Baron de Rivière, and was well-educated, enjoyed good books, and was of very striking appearance with blond hair that he wore fairly long, a moustache, and a goatee that he kept trimmed neatly.

In his youth he had been something of a trial to his family, and his father arranged to have him inducted in the French navy, where he served as a midshipman on a battleship. The ship went on a diplomatic world cruise, which was partly a training exercise for the crew, and in due course stopped at New York. The crew was given a short leave then, and Frenchy, who hated the role of a mere servant to the officers and burned to the marrow of his bones at being subject to the rigid discipline, did not come back. Dressed in a navy uniform and being easy to spot, he was quickly apprehended and brought back. As punishment his arms were lashed tightly behind his back, a brass spittoon was tied in front of him, and he was ordered to stand at the top of the gangplank with his legs in irons. Every man who passed him was under orders to spit in the spittoon and many of them didn't hit it. Frenchy fumed but he managed to get through to a point where he once more was on deck as part of the working crew. But when the ship sailed through the Caribbean and stopped at New Orleans, he waited until after dark one rainy night, stripped, and went overboard. A powerful swimmer, he made his way to shore and into a brothel, where the girls were so intrigued by him that they hid him from the shore patrols searching for him. He must have stayed there for a while – though perhaps not in the brothel – for all his life he spoke with a touch of the soft accent of the south.

He eventually made his way far up the Mississippi and to the great prairie country where he went to work on a big horse ranch in Wyoming. A superb horseman with a natural ability to make friends with the wildest horses and teach them to answer the reins, he had no trouble finding jobs. Eventually, he made his way north to Canada, where he ran into another character by the name of Paddy Hassen, the squaw man who sold his ranch to my grandfather.

It was during the excitement of the gold strikes in the Yukon, and Paddy, recognizing a man who was a genius with horses as well as an adventurer, invited Frenchy to go with him on a venture to trail a bunch of horses north on the Klondike Trail.

The Klondike Trail, though on everybody's lips as the route from Alberta to the diggings at Whitehorse and Dawson City, was really a trail going nowhere. It went from Edmonton north to the Peace River, then west through Grand Prairie, Pouce Coupé, and then across the mighty Peace River to Dawson Creek and Fort St. John. From there it went on north into vast stretches of mountains, jackpine jungle, past Fort Nelson, to lose itself by degrees of enormous difficulty and lack of adequate grass. As far as it went on that leg of its journey, it was one long string of starving men and dead horses. It was pure hell. The stories coming back were so horrendous the North-West Mounted Police organized a well-equipped party to find out if this route was feasible. They had a very bad time and finally gave it up, then came back to Fort St. John and closed the trail.

In the meantime Paddy and Frenchy were on their way north and west from Edmonton with three hundred horses. When they finally arrived at Fort St. John, it was just in time to find the trail closed, so there they were, about a thousand miles this side of Whitehorse. There was nothing for them to do but sell their horses for whatever they could get for them and then the partnership broke up. As part of his share, Frenchy cut out a dozen of the best of the horses to keep for himself, and prepared to take them back to Alberta.

By this time the Peace was in full flood and impossible to cross, but Frenchy was undaunted. He made camp on the river's edge by a big eddy and went to work. The river was full of drifting logs, with many of them circling slowly in the eddy. He had a good supply of rope and proceeded to gather suitable logs to make a raft. At one end of it, he rigged a big sweep to steer it with, and in the middle of it he constructed a pen to hold his horses. When all was ready he launched it, and down the river he went for about one hundred and fifty miles to the settlement of Peace River, where he took his horses ashore and eventually proceeded back to Edmonton.

He was there in 1905 when Alberta became a province. Dressed in his beaded buckskins, Frenchy was a welcome addition to Edmonton society when he came to town, for being fluently bilingual and a gifted raconteur he could mingle with trappers, traders, aspiring socialites, and government officials as well as ranchers and settlers. He was well-read and could talk about any subject, and his background had given him a certain courtly air that was attractive, particularly with the ladies, who inevitably thought he was fascinating.

One of the things the new government proceeded to do was appoint a game commissioner, whose duty it was to organize a fish and wildlife department and give the disappearing fish, furbearers, and big game some badly needed protection. Frenchy had trapped and hunted with the Indians and acquired considerable knowledge of wildlife, so when he heard that the game commissioner planned to hire some game wardens he applied for a job. He was accepted, the first man to become a warden in the province.

It so happened that the commissioner had a problem concerned with a market hunting ring in the St. Paul district about a hundred miles northeast of Edmonton. It was a settlement of French Canadians and Métis (French-Cree halfbreeds), so Frenchy's command of the language was a distinct advantage. Without a great deal of difficulty, he rounded up the culprits, who were duly arrested, tried in court, and fined. In a country where hunting had always been considered a freedom enjoyed by all, this sudden turn of events was not exactly popular, and when Frenchy in his own way proceeded to hunt down and charge more people who were paying no attention to the new Fish and Wildlife Act, he was faced with threats to his life, which he duly reported to the commissioner.

It so happened that a pack of timber wolves was causing considerable losses of horses and cattle in the country just east of the newly formed Waterton Lakes National Park. Frenchy was sent to hunt down the wolves and he arrived there with seven husky dogs in the late fall of 1911.

To allow maximum mobility, he packed his food and camp outfit on the dogsled and proceeded to trail the wolves. He never let up in his pursuit of the pack and they led him on a long trail week after week. When the snow got deep he strapped on a pair of snowshoes and broke trail for his dogs. Once he got a shot with his rifle at one of the wolves and killed it. They never gave him another chance all winter, and come spring, the pack lined out along the foot of the mountains heading north. When the snow melted, he lost their trail and came back to the Pincher Creek country where he took up a homestead on the creek just a couple of miles east of the mountains. In the meantime, he had met Nellie Gladstone and she came to share his cabin. She was a tall, strong, handsome woman who proceeded to give birth to babies with regularity until ten children sat around their table. I knew them all but the two oldest girls, who had married and gone with their husbands by the time I came along. They were tall, handsome people, most of them wild as hawks, able to take care of themselves in about any kind of situation the wilderness chose to throw at them.

I recall Frenchy's method of breaking horses to ride. Every spring he rounded up his bunch of range mares, which were about as wild as horses get. Cutting out the yearlings, he assigned them to his various offspring and it wasn't long before they were gentle. I remember seeing Frances, who was the youngest and about my age, riding to school on one of these young horses. She came on the dead run, bareback, with only a hackamore to guide her mount, her long black braids standing straight out behind her. They were all keen, intelligent youngsters but Frances shared their general dislike of the confines of even a hill-country one-room school. She learned to read and write, but then she was gone back to the mountains.

Charlie, one of the boys, at the age of nine or ten years, was placed in the Catholic school in Pincher Creek, where the children were taught and supervised by nuns. One of them found Charlie sitting on the top step of the back stairs smoking a cigarette. She remonstrated with him in no uncertain terms and told him that cigarettes were bad for him. He agreed and told her he had forgotten his pipe. He hid himself one day under the seat of Harold Butcher's light wagon when he was in town and wasn't discovered till Butcher got back to the ranch. He walked the rest of the way home, and though he attended the local school after this incident, he soon left permanently.

Nellie was close to seventy when she passed away but Frenchy lived to his mid-eighties. They were people of the frontier who saw the prairies and the mountains before they changed and who knew how to live with what was at hand. Victims of racial discrimination because of their Indian blood, they were considered to be ignorant by many of the homesteaders and ranchers, but they were very self-reliant. As far as I know none of them went hungry for very long, and they generally had clothes enough to stay warm in winter.

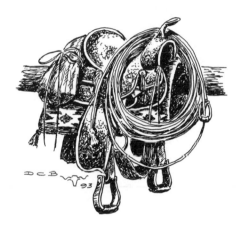

CHAPTER 14

Cows, Cayuses, and Dudes

It was in 1868 that Howard Eaton came west from Pittsburgh, Pennsylvania, by the Northern Pacific train to the end of steel not far east of the Montana border. He was nineteen years old, tall and strong, with an attractive, outgoing personality. No stranger to horses and guns, he was the kind of person who not only looked with a good measure of honest curiosity, but really saw the details of people and country with understanding and more than just a little generosity. He became what might be honestly described as an instant westerner upon being exposed to the huge grand country of the upper Missouri River and its tributaries, virtually uninhabited at that time and, as more than one person remarked, the west was never quite the same again. It had recently been swept clear of the hostile Sioux, who had been assigned reservations following the efforts of the U.S. Cavalry, a move

that was in many ways anything but sympathetic, though generally effective.

When Howard Eaton got off the train at the construction camp marking the end of steel, he had three horses, two to ride and one to pack his camping equipment and other personal gear. For a considerable time, he just rode, looking at this vast expanse of country from horseback and talking to the people he met. He must have been a bit lonesome at times, for he came from a big family. Along with his mother and father there were nine sisters and brothers. His father owned a large dry-goods store in Pittsburgh. Howard and his brothers had spent a good part of their boyhood hunting and fishing in the hills and valleys of back-country Pennsylvania, so they were familiar with wild country.

He was by nature a communicator, so at night by his campfire he took out a notebook and wrote letters to his family and friends describing the country and his experiences, while his horses grazed nearby from their picket ropes.

He was truly in love with this country, particularly the valley and adjoining hills of the Little Missouri River, though his riding took him far afield as well. He rode into the Missouri Breaks, one of the most unique and spectacular regions in the United States, a maze of castellated sandstone towers flanking twisted canyons that wound their tortuous way past mesas and buttes, all shaped and sculpted by wind and water into grotesque shapes – very complicated geography with a grandeur that defied description. As my old friend Jack Reid, who grew up in that country, said, "You could sometimes see a cow close enough to read her brand, but it could take you half a day to get to her."

The Breaks was the home range of deer, elk, and mountain bighorn sheep. Early in the fall of that year Howard found an abandoned cabin on the edge of the Breaks and, with hunting in mind, he proceeded to take it over. He carried a Winchester Model 76 .44 calibre rifle, an accurate weapon, so he not only killed his own meat but also packed out what he didn't use himself to sell to the railroad camps for cash.

His brother Alden joined him there in 1881 and another brother, Willis, came in 1882. Together they hunted game for the railroad-camp kitchens but also contracted to put up hay for the horses of a cavalry post close by. Every bit of cash they could spare was invested in cattle, which they located on the Little Missouri River. At that time all that was needed to claim land was to build a cabin, with some kind of shelter for their saddlehorses, and a corral. The brothers were not afraid of work and it was only a matter of time before they began to receive visitors from Pittsburgh. Howard had spread the word through his letters to friends and relatives. Howard was a born public-relations man, and his visitors had such a good time that they generally stayed much longer than they had planned. They called the place the Custer Trail ranch, because Custer had camped at that spot with his cavalry regiment on one of his patrols prior to the historic massacre on the Little Bighorn River, where the general and all his men were wiped out.

There was nothing fancy about the place, it was just a frontier ranch. Guests slept wherever a bed could be made under some kind of a roof. Sometimes the Custer Trail ranch looked like a tent town. That summer of 1882, a businessman from Buffalo, New York, by the name of Bert Ramsey, came, and he was not only deeply impressed by his experiences there but also aware of the fact that if the Eatons were going to survive, they were going to be forced to charge their guests for the food and services they received. When he reluctantly set about getting ready to leave, he insisted on paying for his holiday, so he became the first paying guest on what was to become the biggest and best-known dude ranch in the United States, if not in the entire world.

The ranch then was a working cow ranch where guests rode with the cowboys. Accommodations were primitive. There was no special entertainment other than sitting around a fire in the evening listening to the stories told by Howard and his brothers. Guests ate bacon, beans, and potatoes with venison or wild mutton, the principal meats. They paid as little as twenty-five dollars a month for the privilege of living on the frontier and they loved it, for they came back again and again.

That year in 1882 the Eatons got a new neighbour, the Marquis de Mores, a colourful man who came from France. He established the beginning of a small town, which he called Medora, after his wife. They were sporting people who loved to hunt and ride with their pack of hounds after coyotes and wolves. The marquis was a flamboyant ambitious type who came up with the idea to build a packing house, which would process meat near the ranches, ship it east under refrigeration, and sell it directly to customers. Refrigeration was supplied by ice taken off the river in winter and stored in big ice houses insulated with sawdust. He proceeded with much building, which included a big stone house. But his business was in direct competition with Swift and Armour's meat business in Chicago, who had enormous stockyards and packing houses as well as an established market reaching all over the eastern and southern United States. In spite of being a very rich man, the Marquis went bankrupt and returned to France.

Another neighbour of the Eatons was Theodore Roosevelt. He owned a sizable ranch, hunted extensively, and of course became the president of the United States. Among the many notable things he did was to mark the boundaries and establish an astonishing number of national parks and national forests in the United States, the most notable being the Yellowstone and Glacier national parks.

During his extensive horseback travels in his first two years in the west, Howard Eaton had ridden up the Yellowstone River along the old immigrant trail, past Immigrant Peak and Mammoth Hot Springs, into the area of Yellowstone Park where geysers roared with thunderous intensity as they heaved columns of hot water, mud, and steam high into the air while the earth trembled under his horses' feet. Colter, the famed mountain man who had originally come west with Lewis and Clark on their historic expedition to the Pacific Ocean in 1804-05, had discovered this place and wintered there all alone and trapped many beaver. When he came out to rendezvous with the fur traders the following summer, he told stories of this fabulous region. The traders instantly gave him the dubious title of the greatest liar in all the Rocky Mountains, and just to secure his position he embroidered his stories with tales of seeing a glass mountain and many other things equally ridiculous but nonetheless very entertaining.

Howard Eaton had seen all these marvels too, and so, in the course of activity around the Custer Trail ranch, he organized a big pack train accompanied by wagons involving two hundred head of horses to take a party of guests through Yellowstone Park. The people who came were totally enthralled with their experience and when they went home they found it difficult to stop talking about their adventures. Some of their stories were published in eastern newspapers and magazines, with the result that the Eatons were snowed under by applications to join his next mountain pack-train trip. It was a long way from the Custer Trail ranch to Yellowstone Park, which created logistical problems, so the Eatons decided to change their ranch location. They sold the Custer

Trail ranch and bought another ranch on Wolf Creek in Wyoming at the foot of the Bighorn Mountains, about thirty miles west and north of the Sheridan. They announced that they would not be booking any guests that year, but it made no difference. Guests showed up anyway to help round up cattle and horses and generally join in and enjoy this historic occasion. Some of the people who joined in this exodus from the Little Missouri country in North Dakota to Wolf Creek never went back, but stayed on to help build the new head-quarters and look after guests. A whole village of little log cabins with roofs of poles, tarpaper, and sod were built.

The place had been originally built to accommodate a sawmill and a flour mill and was never intended to be a cow and horse ranch or to accommodate dudes, but it had been profitable and included a big stone house and a sizable barn. The Eatons lived in the house and converted the well-built barn into an office building. They also purchased another ranch, which they used for a winter horse range.

Breeding horses for use on a dude ranch is not practical, for it takes at least three or four years to raise a horse to matu-rity and more time, depending on the nature of a horse, before it is gentle enough to be ridden safely by green riders from a city environment. So the Eatons bought their good, upstanding gentle mounts all over the west, from as far away as Kansas.

In the course of events Howard went east during the winter to promote a big pack-train expedition north to Glacier Park, Montana. Glacier Park was then relatively undeveloped. A family by the name of Brewster with an out-fitting service in Banff National Park, Alberta, had taken up a concession at East Glacier. To take care of this expansion they bought a string of horses from Frenchy Rivière, who had a ranch south of Pincher Creek, and they hired George Rivière, one of Frenchy's sons, to help trail the horses south to Glacier Park where he was due to gentle the green broke horses at their headquarters there.

Somehow Howard Eaton had oversold his Glacier Park pack-train trip and when he met his party at the railroad station, he found himself short of horses, so he made a deal with the Brewsters for extra mounts and packhorses to cover the needs of his guests.

That was the beginning of what amounted to a disaster, for he got a large part of the horses wearing the Rivière brand that were still so snaky they proceeded to unload dudes and packs all over the country. Fortunately the dudes survived, but some of their belongings were never seen again. Frenchy's horses were mountain-bred. They were not satisfied with getting rid of their riders and loads, but pointed their noses north in the general direction of home. Howard's guests got more than they bargained for, experiencing a considerable amount of very real western atmosphere that summer among Glacier Park's extremely rugged untracked mountains. The whole episode cost the Brewsters so much that they gave up their concession and returned to Banff and Jasper parks in Alberta, where they enjoyed a long and profitable record in the outfitting business over a period of seventy-odd years.

Whatever the trials and tribulations Howard Eaton encountered that year in Glacier Park, they in no way had any negative effect on the Eaton ranch in Wyoming. They proceeded not only to take successful pack trips into the mountains but developed the ranch till it had accommodation for 125 people.

One of Howard's closest friends who regularly came to the ranch was Mary Roberts Rhinehart, the celebrated author. Another was Charlie Russell, the famous cowboy artist. One time Charlie was out hunting with Howard and killed a large mule-deer buck, which they loaded on a horse and then headed for camp. When they got there they found the place had been taken over by a pair of skunks busy raiding their food packs.

Howard sat his horse surveying this somewhat touchy scene and said to Charlie, "You know, I could probably rope 'em and lead 'em out of here, or I could shoot 'em, but I doubt if either idea is much good."

Charlie's face was serious as an owl's as he spent a bit of time contemplating the problem, but his eyes gave away the laughter that was close to the surface. He opined, "You know, Howard, that nobody ever won a wrasslin' match with a skunk. You could kill 'em, but their memory would linger on for a long time, skunk perfume bein' what it is!"

The skunks proceeded to solve the problem by realizing that the neighbourhood was getting unduly crowded. One of them dragged away a piece of bacon to a big badger hole nearby and disappeared into the ground with the other skunk following.

Howard and Charlie proceeded to move camp. Later Charlie made a painting featuring a couple of riders and a packhorse politely waiting for their visitors to leave, which he gave to Howard. For years it occupied a place of honour over the fireplace in the big house. Years later, when they had a forest fire at the ranch that could have wiped out the whole place, but was fortunately brought under control in time, the family got worried about the painting, which had become very valuable. They sold it for considerably more money than had been paid for the ranch. Before it left the place, they had an artist paint a replica, which still hangs over the fireplace in the house.

Howard eventually passed away, but his place was taken by a nephew, "Big" Bill, Alden Eaton's only son, who had grown up on the ranch and taken over as manager. He was running the place in 1955 when I visited it with Jack Reid.

Jack's older brother Wallace had married a young lady by the name of Minnie Brown but then died shortly after from acute appendicitis. Howard Eaton married Minnie later and she was the hostess at Eaton ranch for the rest of her life. She was an old and very charming lady when I was there.

For many years many of the guests on our pack train, which had been running since 1907 under Bert Riggall's ownership, had also visited the Eaton ranch. I worked for Bert for ten years prior to buying the business in 1946 and had an idea in the back of my mind to develop the ranch into a dude ranch. Knowing the Eaton ranch had a great reputation, I was anxious to see it. We were only there for a few days, but it was an unforgettable experience.

Bill Eaton was a big man, very strong and probably the best roper Wyoming ever saw, and that covers a big territory. One trick he used to do at ranch entertainments for the guests, and also one he did at rodeos, was to take a long rope, build a big loop, and throw it standing on edge so that five riders crossing abreast in front of him could run their horses through it. Such a feat with a rope demands tremendous strength.

When I was there, George Gentry was the man in charge of the two hundred horses used as mounts for the guests. I saw the early morning gather of horses come down off the high grassy slopes of the mountains, with the dust banners over various bunches all lit up in the sun as the riders drove them down to the corral.

After dinner the night before a ride, all the guests wishing to ride the next day would leave their names on a list hanging just inside the dining-hall door. The next morning Patti Eaton, Bill's wife, took this list and stood on a ramp just outside the corral gate to call out the numbers as Bill and George took turns riding in and roping the designated horses, each one with a number painted on its rump.

As each one was caught, it was led down to a long tack room where the saddles were hung on racks – saddles that either belonged to the guests or were fitted and assigned to them. There were two saddlers at each entrance door who proceeded to bridle and saddle each horse as it came to them.

The morning that I watched, Bill and George roped sixty-six horses in an hour. Bill used a nylon rope and George had a braided rawhide. There was only one loop missed. One horse dodged a loop thrown by George by putting its head under the belly of another. George quickly built another loop which he closed over the head of the errant horse with an audible snap and the next moment it was heading for the gate.

All in all, that was the finest roping I have ever watched. To catch, lead out, and saddle sixty-six horses in an hour speaks of skill and finely tuned organization. There was no milling or plunging among the horses as they were being caught. It was worth the five-hundred-mile drive just to see.

When I came to realize that their home ranch enclosed seventeen thousand acres of range and that they had grazing access to a million and a quarter acres of National Forest land in addition, I knew that my land was too small even for the horses I would need, let alone the cattle, which are still a very definite part of their operation. So my dude-ranch plan was set aside indefinitely.

The Eaton ranch has a great tradition. It has been in operation for over one hundred years, with the fifth generation of the family now active on it. The number of people who have enjoyed its hospitality are legion, as is the number of people who have come to love and appreciate nature through its influence.

CHAPTER 15

In Retrospect

Away back there when I was a boy there was no kind of entertainment obtainable by merely pushing a switch and watching a screen. A few of us had gramophones and a collection of records. Radio was just in its infancy, black mysterious squawk-boxes that picked up distant stations broadcasting music and drama often almost obliterated by static. On clear nights it was possible to tune into Salt Lake City, Utah, and also Denver, Colorado, which had powerful transmitters. The best Canadian station was CFCN in Calgary, which gave the news and some country-western music enjoyed by all. Radios were expensive, and most of us couldn't afford them.

Most homes had musical instruments of one kind or another and we often gathered to listen to music and sing songs. One's position in the social strata of most communities was mostly dependent on an ability to tell stories about things we had experienced, and these were often well-spiced

DON BRESTLER 93

with humour. I have met men who couldn't write their own names who could have made their living by entertaining in this fashion, although such an idea never entered their heads and the prospect would have horrified them. They were real elocutionists with a flair for speaking in dialects: men who could mimic the British, French, Scottish, and sometimes Indian accents of speech. No story ever lost anything in their telling and their renditions often left their listeners absolutely helpless with laughter. From the time I was a small boy I listened with absolute rapture to an endless round of such stories around evening fires in homes and camps across the hills and in the mountains, and by this exposure to wilderness raconteurs developed my own style of storytelling, which has been a real part of my life. So when I look back on seventy years, it is to recall a host of characters, most of them now in their graves, that I either knew personally or heard about, who all contributed to the history of this big land. Many of them never accumulated more worldly goods than could be packed on the back of a horse without overloading it, some of them were a bit careless about the law, but nearly all of them had the virtue of showing up to help and cheer somebody in trouble when they needed it. Many of them were real princes disguised in frontier clothing, the unforgettable kind always ready to share a laugh or whatever else they had.

Given time and exposure, it didn't usually matter how green a man was when he started; he learned how to cope with cow-country environment and generally acquired enough skill to hold down a job.

There were exceptions, of course. One young Englishman got a job on one of the big ranches but didn't last long. In the course of events, he was sent to a holding pasture to cut out eleven four-year-old steers and came back with four eleven-year-old cows. He was quickly looking for another job. When somebody asked him what had happened, he explained, "I couldn't remember whether the boss said eleven four-year-olds or four eleven-year-olds. I made a bit of an error, you see. By Jove, he was frightfully unreasonable about it! He fired me!"

My grandfather hired a young man from Toronto who came to the ranch looking for work. He was the son of a manufacturing tycoon and very enthusiastic but, of course, very green. He was, as Grandfather put it, "so green that a cow would likely have chewed on him if he stood still in one place for too long."

He was relegated to being general chore boy and one of the first jobs Grandfather gave him was to grease a wagon. He came back with the empty grease can half an hour later to report that there wasn't enough grease – there had only been enough, he said, "to do the seat"!

Another day, he was instructed to dig a hole for a new gatepost at the corral. "Be sure to dig it good and deep," Grandfather told him, as he rode out to gather some horses. The horses were hidden and the ride was somewhat longer than expected. When he got back, dirt was still flying out of a large hole in the sandy soil and his new employee was just about out of sight. "It would have been all right if my post had been long enough," my grandfather remarked in recalling the incident years later. History does not record whether this one ever graduated to being a cowboy.

It is generally recognized that cowboys are a physically tough breed. One old-timer remarked that it is hard to kill one: "About the only way to be sure is to cut off his head and hide it someplace where he can't find it." Certainly they have been known to survive some awesome injuries.

One, Guy Pallister by name, was helping load some four-year-old beef steers at Cayley, Alberta, in 1907. The crew loaded a boxcar and Guy was putting the "bull bar" across the door, when a wild steer cut loose and struck him. The sharp horn opened him like a knife and when the dust settled there was Guy all doubled up trying to hold his insides in with his hands. The train engine was ready to go, so the cowboys loaded him in the caboose and they headed for High River. There the doctor rearranged Guy's innards and sewed him up. By the following spring he was back working at the Oxley ranch. He later married, and when he died in 1958, at age eighty-five, he was survived by ten sons and three daughters.

One of the toughest, most colourful and eccentric old cowboys I ever met was "Barbwire" John Spears, who was born in Manitoba in 1890 and moved west to Fort Macleod with his family when he was ten years old. When he was only fourteen, he quit school and went to work. It is doubtful if Johnny ever knew the meaning of real fear, though, as he said, he was sometimes a bit scared and he knew how to be cautious when the occasion called for it. He was still in his teens when he worked as a rough rider on various ranches, some as far away as Oregon, breaking horses that a lot of men wouldn't care to lead to water.

He showed up one day at the Waldron ranch, dressed in mismatched boots and ragged clothes, down on his luck and looking for a job, claiming he could handle rough horses. The foreman wished to be rid of this ragged, yet insistent kid, so he cut out an outlaw for him to gentle. He didn't even give him a saddle before taking his crew out to work some cattle, leaving Johnny alone in the corral with the horse.

"It didn't take me long to size up that ol' booger," Johnny told me years later. "He was meaner'n cat piss! He had a glass eye on one side an' a half-chewed-off ear on the other, and the way he stood there at the end of my rope, chuckin' his head with rollers in his nose, I knowed he wanted to kill me!"

Johnny snared the horse's front feet with another rope and hobbled him. Then he tied up a hind foot to his shoulder and worked the outlaw over with an old cowhide that was hung on the fence. When the horse quit fighting the ropes, Johnny went looking for a saddle. All he could find was a pack saddle and two old stirrups that didn't match, which he rigged up with a couple of lengths of rope. He cinched the makeshift outfit down on the horse and tied an old sheepskin on to it for a seat. All the while the horse was just standing there waiting for Johnny to get on top of him.

This is what Johnny had in mind, but first he gathered up some pieces of scrap iron from around the place and tied them to the saddle with pieces of rope that were long enough to give the scraps some room to play. Then he took the hobbles off the horse and stepped back to give him some space.

"He took a step, then blew up and went buckin' around the corral kickin' and swappin' ends with that iron bangin' him, but he weren't no fool, that horse. He came to a stop chuckin' his head and blowin' his nose at me, just darin' me to get up on him. This I was fixin' to do, but first I went down to the creek and cut me a willer about three foot long and an inch through. When I hit that saddle, he came apart high, wide, and handsome, like he was tryin' to kick me out from under my hat. I caught him a lick over the nose with that willer. That, on top of the iron bangin' him, was too much, and he quit. I moved him over to the gate and opened it and headed down the valley where the crew was workin' cattle. They was some surprised to see me on that horse with all that iron decoratin' him. He knew about workin' cattle, but got mad once in a while and tried to bite a piece out of my leg, but the willer put a stop to that!"

Johnny stayed in that country, took up a homestead, and eventually got married. They had one daughter, who was grown up when Johnny and his wife had a serious difference of opinion over the attentions being paid by another man. His wife went to the police along with her friend and signed a warrant to have Johnny declared insane.

Johnny got wind of this move and when he saw the police car coming, he rode out to meet it bareback on a bony old workhorse, waving the naked spokes of a broken umbrella over his head and wearing only the heavy growth of hair that covered most of his body. Naturally the police had no choice but to take him into custody and to the mental hospital.

Johnny's idea of humour had backfired in a way that would have discouraged most men beyond reason. However, he was a model patient, helping everyone he could, cheerful, entertaining, and totally cooperative. He was there about a year when the doctors in charge held a meeting to review his case. They unanimously agreed that he might be eccentric but he was certainly of healthy mind, so they gave him a certificate saying as much and Johnny headed back to the hills and mountains. I rode with him helping gather some cattle one fall when he told me this story, and to wind it up, he unpinned the flap of his shirt pocket and took out a piece of paper carefully wrapped in some waterproofed silk. It was the certificate of sound mental health.

"They called me crazy," he stated, "but I'm the only guy you'll likely ever see who ain't and has the proof!"

One rainy day when he was in his seventies, Johnny was riding and keeping an eye on a bunch of cattle up on the Livingstone River, the north fork of the Oldman. A grizzly showed up, which Johnny suspected of killing a cow, and Johnny sallied forth and shot it. By the time he got back to the cabin, he was tired and soaked to the hide, so he hauled the bear into the cabin, intending to skin it when it was dry. When he had eaten his supper, he made the mistake of lying down for a while on his bunk and when he woke up it was morning. It was warm in early June and the bear had swelled up to a point where he couldn't get it back out the door, so he stripped off and proceeded to skin it.

The Forestry Department was building a road, which had reached the cabin, and, it being a weekend, some enterprising city explorers drove up to the cabin. They saw smoke coming out of the stovepipe and in due course walked over to the open door and looked in. There was Johnny, naked as the day he was born, busy skinning the bear. After one look and no doubt a sniff of air that was so rank it brought tears to their eyes, the man and his wife hastily retreated to their vehicle and departed. Thus another "Barbwire" Johnny Spears story was born. Johnny has gone to his grave long since, but nobody who knew him will ever forget him.

The old-timers' methods of gentling wild range horses were largely of the rough and ready school of thinking; they were first halter-broke, ridden enough in a corral to start them answering the rein, and then put to work. But there were some men who had different methods.

Years ago, when I owned over a hundred head of saddle- and packhorses used in my mountain outfitting business, it seemed that in spite of plans to the contrary I always had a few snakes in the bunch. One day a man named Frank Moon showed up looking for work and claimed to have some experience gentling horses. He was about sixty years old, had a look about him of having spent a lot of time in the saddle, but unlike a lot of old bronc fighters, he showed no signs of being stove up, so I hired him.

Next morning we corralled a bunch of horses, and among them were two line-back buckskin mares – full sisters, strong, good-looking horses that were ideal for mountain work. I had bought them along with a bunch of other horses, but whoever had handled them had abused them and they were the meanest kickers I have ever seen – the cool, calculating kind that are really dangerous. My plan was to sell them to a pet-food cannery, for if there is any horse I hate to have around, it is a kicker. On a dude outfit they are dynamite in disguise, especially this kind; they just wait for a chance then let drive with one or both hind feet, trying to wipe a man out.

As I showed the horses to Frank, I told him about these mares and my plans for them, and also that he didn't have to work with them. He stood there for a while looking them over and just grunted a reply. I left him and headed for the house where I had some desk work to do. About half an hour later, he showed up at the door and asked me to come out for another look at one of my mean buckskins. I found one of the mares standing alone in the round bronc corral with a lariat on her head and the rest of it coiled neatly on the ground in front of her.

"This horse is plumb gentle," he told me and then to prove it, he walked up behind her, took hold of her tail, and gave it a pull. Getting down on his hands and knees, he crawled under her belly by squeezing through between her hind legs and out between her front ones. Then he stood up, talked to her in a low voice, and rubbed her ears. She obviously loved it. Hardly able to believe what I had been seeing, I took a closer look at the hitch on her head. It was a simple nerve-line hitch rigged in a way I had never seen before.

A nerve line is rigged to work on two pressure points just back of a horse's ears, where two major nerves come closer to the skin, and is used not only to distract the animal from struggling but also to bring it under positive control. When not used properly, such a hitch can ruin a horse, but Frank was a master of the technique.

Next day he called me out to the corral again, and again he had the mare by herself, this time completely free with no halter or lead rope. He had a light buggy-whip in his hand and, laying it across her back, he spoke to her and she trailed along beside him like a pet dog as he walked. Taking her to the back of the barn, he opened the door and took her through it, commanded her to stop, walked around behind her and closed the door, then led her down behind a line of stalls full of horses and out another door into the open yard. There I wouldn't have been surprised if she had made a break for freedom, but she seemed to be mesmerized. She followed him around the yard in a big circle before he walked her back through the barn following the same routine of opening and closing doors.

The next week she and her sister joined my pack train for a summer and fall in the mountains. Both were model horses, easy to catch and friendly, as was every bronc that Frank trained. He had worked all his life on ranches scattered from Alberta to Texas, and as far as I know no horse ever bucked with him. I once heard him say that if you wanted to teach a horse anything, you had to know a bit more than the horse. He died in his late eighties and Alberta lost one of the finest horse tamers and trainers that ever lived in the west.

I met and worked with a lot of cowboys over the years. Some of them stand out very distinctly from the rest and one of these was Ralph Vroom. Ralph could be as wild as they got. He lived with the law but not always within it. He would give a friend his shirt if that friend needed it but, given reason, he could be an implacable, dangerous enemy. He wasn't very big as men go but he was tough, colourful, and a showy rider without being a show-off, though he loved to entertain people. He could get on and off a horse like a flash, never seeming to touch a stirrup.

He had a good-looking palomino stud that he rode on special occasions and I remember him coming into Pincher Creek one time riding this horse that he had trained to buck. He was wearing a pair of angora batwing chaps dyed orange with black spots, and with his big hat, embroidered vest, and silver-mounted bit and spurs, he made quite a picture as he rode the prancing horse down Main Street. All of a sudden the horse blew up and Ralph went over his head to come down on all fours in front of his horse making great buck jumps with the horse trailing and bucking behind him. Then like magic Ralph was back in the saddle, the horse never missing a step as it pranced on down the street heading for the livery barn.

I was out in Yarrow Creek Valley one day riding a bronc when I met Ralph trailing in the lead of a string of horses with his son Bill bringing up the rear. He was heading for Waterton Park where he planned to set up a trail-riding service for the summer. He and Bill were both riding broncs and they had ten horses between them – all broncs with only one gentle mare carrying a pack. The mare was travelling with difficulty and was obviously sick.

"She was fine when we started this morning," Ralph told me, "but then she started to sweat a bit back up the trail. What do you think could be wrong with her?"

"No way to tell," I told him, "but she looks like she's going to die."

At that moment the mare keeled over with a crash and was dead when she hit the ground.

"I got a problem," Ralph said. "These horses are still pretty wild and its goin' to be somethin' else to catch one out here on this flat."

We bunched them up and I roped one. My horse started to buck but quit when the gelding hit the end of the rope. Then Ralph and I proceeded to hobble, blindfold, and saddle the bronc while Bill held our horses. I was coming up quietly on one side of it with a pack-box full of tools, horseshoes, and cooking gear, while Ralph walked up on the other side and set the box against the saddle with a rattle of similar stuff. The horse jumped so high straight up that I could see Ralph standing there holding the box waiting for it to come down.

"I guess we're goin' to have to play this pretty easy," he opined as the horse quit trying for altitude. We did and, when we got it packed, he got back on his horse and I passed him the halter shank so he could lead it. The packhorse jumped and the pack rattled, whereupon Bill and I had a good view of Ralph's horse and it bucking out across the flat, with all that tin and iron keeping time. We finally got everything back in control and proceeded on our way. I left them at the ranch gate, but I was wondering how they were going to find dudes tough and able enough to ride those horses on mountain trails.

But a week or so later we were camped with our pack outfit up at Twin Lakes on the near side of the Great Divide when Bill showed up all alone with a family party – a man, his wife, and kids all riding those same broncs and getting along fine. I wouldn't have believed it if I hadn't seen it.

But I had seen and heard enough of Ralph and horses to believe just about anything. When he was courting Molly, his wife, and she agreed to marry him, he bought a fancy buggy and driving harness and then looked over his horses to pick a suitable team for the occasion. His pick was a matched pair of five-year-old chestnut mares that had silver manes and tails. The only thing wrong with them was that they weren't even halter-broke and the wedding was only two days away. That, and the fact that Molly's mother and father weren't too happy with their daughter marrying such a wild man, was a bit of a problem, but it never even slowed Ralph down.

He halter-broke the mares, harnessed them, and tied them in his barn for the night. Early in the morning he hitched them up to his wagon and by evening he had them answering the rein after a fashion. Next day, dressed in his finest from big hat to polished boots, he hitched his new team up to the buggy in the corral. After a circle or two around it, he opened the gate and away he went on the dead run heading for Molly's home to pick her up and then take her to the parson who was due to perform the ceremony.

When he came in through her yard gate, she was all dressed with her suitcases packed waiting for him. There was no way he could safely leave that team for a moment, so he made a circle pausing long enough to pick up her luggage and then another circle, this time stopping the horses for a moment to give him time to reach down and pick her up to set her on the seat beside him.

Thus Molly came to live in a cabin on a mountain homestead. It might have been what is known as isolated, but life with Ralph was never dull even if it might have been a bit difficult at times. She was ever gentle – a wonderful mother of their fine family – two daughters and two sons who grew up to make good use of their lives. Living on a homestead in those hills and keeping children fed and clothed was never easy for anyone, but Ralph and Molly managed it well.

Ralph had a keen sense of humour and sometimes went to considerable lengths to play a joke. One of his neighbours was a man by the name of Prigg, a retired military man of the British army who had served in India and was now the local forest ranger. He was also game warden in the Forest Reserve and had a kind of running feud with Ralph, who, he knew, was not averse to eating venison out of season.

One day Prigg saddled his horse to go to town. On the way he met Ralph and, in the course of the conversation, he offered to bring Ralph's mail. As they parted Ralph opined that it would be a good day for him to go get some meat. Prigg rode thoughtfully on down the trail, worrying a bit if Ralph really meant what he said. His suspicion built up till he finally turned around and went back toward home. Sure enough, there were fresh horse tracks over his on the trail and they went on past the ranger station.

Prigg followed and the tracks gave him a merry chase till he finally lost them in spite of much riding in circles trying to pick them up. Meanwhile, Ralph circled back and shot a fat doe licking on the salt block Prigg had set out for his horses. When the ranger got back to his cabin it was dark, and when he went to open the door his hand encountered something that startled him. He struck a match, to find the female part of the doe stretched over the knob, a discovery which made him absolutely furious and spoilt his sleep that night.

Prigg was out on the trail heading for town before daylight and came back with the local Mounted Police officer, who had a search warrant. Ralph was duly surprised, polite, and cooperative while professing great innocence of even thinking of poaching deer out of season, let alone a doe which was protected all year around. A very thorough and painstaking search revealed absolutely nothing to incriminate him and once more Prigg went home feeling thwarted, angry, and generally out of sorts, for while this was not the first time he had tried to catch Ralph, it was particularly galling for obvious reasons. He swore a mighty oath to catch Ralph some day, but when he finally retired that pleasure had never been realized.

Ralph was a really good cowboy and one of the best bronc riders I ever knew. He rode by balance and often won some prize money at local rodeos. I saw him make a money ride one time at the Castle River Stampede, but when the pick-up man went to help him off the horse, his spur hung up on his saddle and he got into a bad wreck that broke his thigh. He was in his late fifties at the time, well past the usual age for contest riding, and it took considerable time before he could step up on a horse again. He never rode at a rodeo from that time on as far as I know. When I saw him last, he was an old man living his late years at the senior citizens' home in

Pincher Creek, but the flame of his enthusiasm for life was bright as ever. This country doesn't make his kind any more but there are still a few such men with us.

Jim Commodore is a living legend at a time when computers, electronics, and such trappings of our culture rule the world. He can tell what a cow says to her calf and what she is likely to do in a given situation before she even thinks of it herself. If I could turn back the calendar to about 1876 and there was a herd of three thousand or so cattle down in Texas that I wanted here, I would go to Jim. He could find the crew and bring them north through all the hazards of floods and drought, hostile Indians, buffalo, and distance that the Great Plains could throw at him. I would happily gamble the price of the herd that he would arrive on time with the cattle in good shape, and any Indians that had tried to take them away from him along his backtrail would have some stories to tell around their evening fires about a white man who was a brave warrior.

Jim was born in the great prairies of southern Saskatchewan and grew up fast in what is probably the toughest climate, save the Arctic, found in all Canada.

His father was a great cowboy and his mother is certainly no stranger to cows and horses, a strong, handsome woman of great courage whom I sometimes have the privilege to meet and trade talk with. Mabel Commodore will do to ride the river with any time; her seventy-four years are a collection of charm.

When Jim was only fifteen, he was making his living working with cows and horses in that big short-grass country of Saskatchewan. That is saying something, for horses that grew up on short-grass range are not particularly famous for being house pets. They are big and strong and have a definite tendency to blow up without much excuse. Away back when the first trail herds of longhorns came north from Texas into

Alberta and Saskatchewan, the cayuses they rode tended to be small though very tough. When they were turned loose on this prairie range, they grew even though they might be five to seven years old, and all of them put on muscle and weight. Any youngster holding down a man's job had to be able to ride.

Jim and a friend of his, another youngster about seventeen years old, took on a job breaking horses at a camp on a big ranch. The horses were very wild, big and strong. What one didn't think of by way of hellery another did, and after a couple of weeks both of the young riders were feeling sore in so many places, they lost count. Jim recalls getting up one morning to light the fire and make some coffee. His partner started rolling out of his bunk and paused to think it over. Looking at Jim, he asked, "Can you please tell me what leg I was limpin' on yesterday?"

They were learning, the horses were learning, and by the end of the summer all and sundry had graduated without any broken bones.

Some of the big ranches had a collection of spoiled horses that might look fine until somebody undertook to do a day's work on them. They never missed a chance to give a cowboy a bad time.

Jim went to work on such an outfit. His string of saddlehorses were known far and wide for their meanness, but he prevailed with them to keep their minds on their business as he rode all alone on a big piece of prairie looking after a sizable herd of cattle. Occasionally he ran into another cowboy, who inquired after his health and looked askance at the horse he rode, obviously a little amazed that Jim was still in one piece. It was there that he rode over the edge into what has grown into a truly great reputation as a man who could get a tough job done anywhere he ran into one.

Today Jim Commodore is manager of a big range in

southern Saskatchewan. Many's the time I have sat with a cup of coffee listening to his stories of his experiences – enough to fill a book by themselves. It is to know that here is one who has been up the creek and over the mountain with no need to embellish fact with fantasy. His trails have taken him from the Saskatchewan and Alberta prairies, foothills, and mountains as far south as the Mexican border, and his accounts of experiences are laced with a sense of humour typical of the cowboy who enjoys what he has done and what he is doing – a man who can laugh at himself. He doesn't suffer fools very long but he has a generous heart. One only has to see him sitting his horse working cows to know that here is a real stockman with a deep, deep love of the land, one of the disappearing few, who is a living example of a longstanding tradition in cowboy culture through the history of the breed.

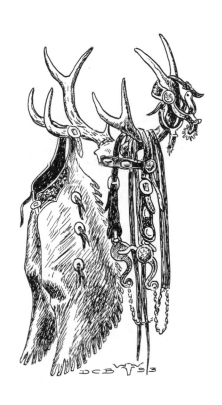

The Wall-Eyed Stud

One evening I was visiting Ralph Vroom at his camp near Red Rock Canyon in Waterton Park. We were sharing a small cheerful fire at the edge of the timber above the creek. It was a perfect night with the stars coming out in the clear vault of the sky and as usual at such a time we were trading stories.

Ralph was sitting with his back to a log, his feet crossed and tucked up close in an attitude of complete relaxation, but as always alert to everything. There was the sound of a tree frog chirping. From down the canyon, a quarter-mile away, a great horned owl was hooting. We both heard a twig snap in the trees behind us and lifted our heads to see a mule-deer doe with two spotted fawns come out on to the meadow to feed while her offspring began to jump and play.

"Cute little rascals," Ralph murmured, "like my kids when they're blowin' off steam."

We watched as the fawns suddenly converged on their mother and began to suckle with their tails wagging back and forth in satisfaction.

In those days there were hundreds of feral horses running wild along both sides of the Great Divide where the Rockies formed the boundary between Alberta and British Columbia. They wore no brands and except for a few – mares that had been stolen from ranchers and Indians by the stallions – belonged to nobody. For a while Ralph just sat there looking at nothing in particular from under his hat brim.

Then he looked at me and said, "It was years ago, when I was single and full of ideas about seein' what was up the creek and over the mountain and how to make a few bucks without takin' orders from nobody. I'd heard there was lots of wild horses in the East Kootenai country around Cranbrook in B.C., so one fine spring day, I put a pack on a big black mare that went by the name of Jinny and saddled my top horse, Ol' Baldy, and headed west through the mountains. It weren't very long before I was lookin' back at Crowsnest Pass. It was an early spring that year and the water was high when I come to the Kootenai River, where they were just finishing a new bridge. I bought enough grub at Cranbrook to top off my supplies, and headed north. The St. Mary's River was runnin' pretty wild, so I played it smart and crossed the railway bridge on the open ties. Very near got run over by a train, but made it to the far side with dry feet. Headin' west for a ways I came up on a ridge overlookin' the Canal Flats country to the east on the headwaters of the Columbia River. Along the way here and there I found horse tracks and saw a few bunches, but it was in a big burn and not very good for tryin' to trap horses, so I kept goin'. It was mighty pretty with lots of new grass. I was goin' up a creek through some mighty fine country with lots of meadows on the bottom and along the mountain sides, when the wind switched to the north and fog blew in in long stringers that hid everything. The way it does sometimes the sky just split open and the rain came down like under a waterfalls. I was lookin' for a place to camp when a cabin showed up. It was old and hadn't been used for years, but it had a good tight roof made of split logs and there was plenty of firewood stacked up under the overhang in front. So I just moved in.

"It wasn't long before I knew I was not alone. All the mice in the valley along with a packrat or two had beat me to it. All night the mice had foot races over me. Some was trying to give me a haircut, and the packrats was makin' as much noise as a herd of horses.

"Next morning, it stopped rainin' and I was sittin' outside thinkin' about movin' camp away from all the livestock, when a weasel showed up from under a log out on the flat. So I sneaked over to sit under a big tree to watch. That weasel was sure busy huntin' for dinner, and it wasn't long before he run over to look around the cabin. That night I heard mice yellin' about a bandit that was murderin' their relatives. Then it got real quiet – even the packrats was makin' no noise. I was makin' breakfast when the weasel poked his head through a knot hole in the floor. He sure looked well-fed and slick. I told him he was welcome to stay.

"The weather was shapin' up to clear, and so I saddled up Ol' Baldy and rode up the valley for a look-see with Jinny trailin' behind. I had thought some about takin' a mare along on a horse huntin' trip, but those two horses couldn't stand to be apart and they both would stay with me in strange country.

"A few miles up the creek, I angled up the side of the valley across some 'steep meadows between some strips of timber when some fresh horse tracks showed up that was about a day old. There was four of 'em – an ol' mare with a new colt, a yearlin', and what I took to be a young stud. They'd been hangin' out on that slope for quite a while and I saw a couple of places where he'd emptied his gut several times in the same place. I'd have bet money the mare was gimpy on her right front leg by the way her tracks was showin'. That meant there was only one horse that was interestin' and maybe he was ugly as sin. Like you know, not very many wild horses are very pretty. Most every horse hunter dreams of findin' some that are special. If I was goin' to trail some horses out of here, I wanted two or three good ones. But I kept goin' and finally tracked this little bunch up onto a timbered bench on top of a hogback ridge. There was no sign of the horses, but their tracks was a lot fresher.

"There was a big ol' red fir growin' there with well-spaced branches all the way to the top so I tied up my horse and climbed it. Lightnin' had hit the top of it sometime and the wind had blown it away, so there was a good place to sit with my toes hooked on branches. The view from that perch was made for eagles. I could see clear across east of the Columbia River to the snowy range of mountains on the far side. I was there maybe half an hour before I saw a horse come out from behind some timber in a basin below on the far side of the ridge. It was a black mare with a mouse-coloured colt and a bay yearlin'. I was right about the mare; she was not very young and she was lame in her right shoulder – it was an old injury and it didn't bother her much. She was slick and fat. Then the fourth horse walked out into the meadow and I damn near fell out of the tree! He was sooty black with a silver mane and tail. His mane grew down to the point of his shoulder and his tail was close to brushin' the ground and they was white as snow. He was built like a dream. But he wasn't movin' right and looked like maybe he'd taken a bad fall or been in a fight with another stud.

"I had to get closer, so I climbed down out of my tree, left my horses, and headed down the slope toward the bottom of the basin, takin' my time. The wind was right so they wouldn't smell me comin'.

"Down near the bottom the ground was flattenin' out but the timber was thick, and not wantin' to walk out too close to them, I stopped to look around. Fifty yards away there was another big fir tree and I pussyfooted over to it. Like the other one, it had lots of branches and it didn't take me long to climb it. I was in luck, for I wasn't much over a hundred yards from the horses.

"They was all grazin' and that stud was something to cure sore eyes, though it was plain to see he had been in a big mix-up with another stud. He had tooth marks all over. The part of him that really got to me was those glass eyes. He had a narrow white stripe on his nose, but his eyes was set in black hair. I'd seen lots of wall-eyed horses and sometimes they're downright ugly, but this one's eyes shone like jewels. I'd never in my life seen a horse like this. One thing was for sure. I had to have that stud.

"When I got back to the cabin, the sun was goin' down. I had a good feed and went to bed. For a long time, I couldn't sleep for thinkin' about that stud. Then I did drop off. I dreamed about him – saw him runnin' in circles, buckin' and playin' like a colt with his tail and mane streamin' in the wind like white flags. When he come gallopin' like he was goin' to run me down, I woke up. That night I found some old wire behind the cabin and added a piece of it to my gear.

"It was still dark the next mornin' when I rode out to find those horses. Ol' Baldy and Jinny was full of grass and feelin' good and we made good time back to where we'd left them. They were gone. But it wasn't because anything had spooked 'em. They had just got itchy feet and was hankerin' for some new scenery like horses do. I didn't mind. I was all primed up to trail 'em clear to the Pacific Ocean if that was what it took to get 'em into a place where I could build a trap to catch and hold 'em. It was gettin' on for late afternoon when we caught up and spooked 'em into a run that took 'em out of sight in the trees in a few jumps. I didn't push 'em but just poked along behind followin' their trail. That ol' mare was in the lead with the stud bringin' up the rear. Most places their tracks was plain, but when they weren't Ol' Baldy took over, sniffin' tracks like a big dog.

"I knowed we was all set to see some country, wild-horse style, and sooner or later there would be a place where I could set up a trap. One night it rained – a real gully-washer. Next mornin' there wasn't any tracks or scent. That mare sure fooled me that day, for she changed direction. I spent some time lookin' where she wasn't and it was afternoon before I spotted a place where the grass was cropped off and it wasn't long before I found fresh tracks headin' up the creek into some country that looked just right for goats.

"I made camp on a meadow and was on their trail again as soon as I could see. The trail was old with blazes showin' here and there that had been made by Injuns. Me and my horses were comin' up to where the creek started with a high ridge behind that looked impossible for horses with steep rock showin' here and there and loose shale in between, but the horse tracks kept goin'. The trail went over a little ridge about timberline so I stopped for a look. There was no sign of the horses beyond their tracks under Ol' Baldy's nose. The big ridge set up ahead of me looked a mile high, but I knew it wasn't as steep as it looked, for a slope with loose shale on it'is never that steep, as you know. But it was sure a long way up to the skyline.

"What looked like a big game trail was cuttin' across a stretch of loose shale near the bottom into a shallow draw between a couple of rock outcrops. Then I saw somethin' movin' and damn if it wasn't those horses! They was makin' slow goin' of it, but they was gainin' on it and headin' for the top. For a while it looked like they was in trouble where the trail went up between those outcrops. They stopped for quite a while, but they was only catchin' their wind, for the ol' mare made a little jump and caught her footin' on a ledge, moved along it a ways and then skipped up on to another to cross a little gully with the colts and the stud trailin' her. It took some time, but they finally topped out against the sky over a mile away by eagle trail and more than that by the way they went.

"I rode down into a shallow basin across another little creek and camped in a scattered grove of big ol' tamaracks to give the horses a chance to rest and feed before we tackled that ridge.

"Ol' Baldy snorted loud enough to wake me up just as the sun came up next mornin'. The first thing I saw was four big muley bucks pokin' around as they sized up my camp. Their horns was all stubby with velvet. I never moved as the biggest one came sneakin' up to my bed. Maybe he had never seen a man before, for he started lickin' at my boots close enough I could have reached out and touched him. He was after salt where the tops had rubbed against my horse. When he started lickin' the tarp coverin' my bed I said 'Good mornin',' and he about turned himself inside out gettin' out of there.

"After breakfast I took the saddle blankets that had been hangin' all night on a rope to dry out a bit and worked them over a log to soften them up before saddlin' my horses.

"I figured it was an old Injun trail, for it hadn't been used for a long time except by the wild ones like goats, deer, and elk. There were places where the shale had slid into it and filled it up, so we lost a step out of about every three. I walked in a lot of places, for the goin' was about as tough as it could get for horses. It was hot as an oven on the front of that ridge and there was no water. It must have taken all of three hours before we hit the summit. About the first thing I saw as me and the horses stood there heavin' for breath was an old bleached-out horse skull. Some pore old Injun horse's heart must have played out on that climb. The view off the top was enough to pay for it.

"That was a piece of the Happy Huntin' Ground! There was a creek comin' down off a stretch of open timberline in a big curve around a mountain that was standin' alone. It curved around into big timber and kept on past another high mountain across the valley where it run into the top end of a lake mostly hidden by the mountain in front of me. It looked like there was another pass up on the head of the creek. Here and there on the higher peaks there was blue ice shinin' where glaciers hung in the pockets. In one place there was a falls comin' out from under the ice that fell like a lace curtain wavin' in the breeze for maybe two thousand feet. I stepped up on my saddle to ride down for a closer look.

"The trail went straight down for a ways into some big timber, where we found a spring and had a good drink. From there I rode along a big ledge of solid rock, down a break and back on another ledge where the trail took off downslope into the timber. There was an old blaze or two there – Injun-made – that was grown in a long ways.

"Ol' Baldy had his nose workin' on the fresh tracks and I watched the country around. In about an hour the trail broke out of the trees where a big avalanche had tore a swath all the way from timberline to the creek. We went through another stretch of timber and out into the open valley along the slope of the creek, which was roarin' down over some big rock ledges like a giant stairs. There was scrub trees and acres and acres of meadows all covered with flowers about every colour in the rainbow. When it come to huntin' country those Injuns knew how to pick her!

"We climbed over a little hogback ridge and come out

above a little basin below some scrubby tamarack timber and there was a flock of about twenty goats busy lickin' at the mud of a big seep that stunk of sulphur. My horse let out a snort that spooked them and they went runnin' up the side of the mountain with the rags of their winter coats floppin' and flutterin'. A quarter of a mile farther up, there was a good campin' place on a little bench under a rock ledge and a clump of shintangle.

"I was bent down gettin' some grub out of the pack, when a nice fat two-year-old muley buck showed up among some rocks as big as cabins across the creek. My grub was gettin' low, so I grabbed my old .45 Colt six-shooter and crawled over behind a rock and waited. When he come on down to the creek for a drink, I was all set with my gun snugged down on top of my hat restin' on the rock. At the shot, the buck dropped in his tracks.

"It took me two days to smoke-dry a whole sack of jerky. I made a new saddle blanket out of the hide. Then early one mornin' I saddled up and rode up the valley towards the head of the creek. Big snowdrifts was meltin' where they had piled up durin' the winter. I saw lots of deer, mostly bucks, and more goats. What looked like a pass was cut off on the far side by a cliff that dropped straight down two or three thousand feet toward the lake. There was no way that old mare and her bunch could get out in that direction, so I rode back down the creek past camp and found their tracks crossin' toward that big mountain. The trail climbed up on a bench among scattered boulders big as houses with grass and scrub trees growin' in between. It was an old game trail and it led up to the foot of a wide ledge that curved up the face of a cliff above a canyon that came down off the mountain through some timber. That ledge was sure well-hidden, for it was hard to see from below until I was right on it. It was wide and smooth enough to ride up with no trouble.

"There was a kind of fold in the mountain where the creek came down off the lower rim of what looked like a big basin. I tied my horses there, took off my boots and put on a pair of moccasins that was in one of my saddle pockets. They was the kind the Stoney Indians use for huntin'. They was made out of elkskin and soled with the spongy hide cut from the neck of a billy goat. Those soles are tough as leather ever gets, and about three quarters of an inch thick. They are quiet to walk with and hold on rock like rubber.

"I quit the trail and climbed around the end of the cliff up on to broken rock and scrub to the top of a ridge overlookin' the basin. I couldn't see much at first but went on along the rim to a point of rock that was higher. From there I could see the whole basin and it was sure pretty, with lots of grass. At first I couldn't see the horses, but then they walked into sight out of a little draw. They'd sure found a piece of heaven that was like a big bowl with one side busted out. There was lots of feed and water well-hidden with no flies. Then a big she-grizzly with two little cubs walked out of a patch of shin-tangle away up the slope on the far side. She was grazin' just like the horses while the cubs rolled and tumbled in play all around her.

"Keepin' out of sight, I circled the basin first to make sure there was no other way out on the far side. The whole rim dropped away in a series of cliffs like steps goin' down toward the creek and the lake, where only goats could travel. That suited me just fine; the horses had only one way out.

"The grizzly and her family were on the move headin' down toward the creek past the horses, but they didn't pay much attention to her. I saw the mare lift her head to watch her, but she didn't move.

"Circling back to my horses, I rode back down the trail. At a place where it narrowed down about four feet wide, I blocked it with a couple of old dry snags and some loose rock, just to be sure the wild ones couldn't sneak out past my camp. I hung my slicker on a stick right in the middle of it and then rode on.

"When I got down close to the bottom, I was lookin' down into the boulders on the bench and there, not more than six jumps from where the trail came to flat ground, was a little circle of grass about sixty feet across with the big rocks makin' a natural fence. A bit on the other side was a good spring. All I had to do was fill the gaps between the boulders with brush and poles and I had my trap corral.

"It took me four days from dawn till dark buildin' that corral. All the tools I had was my axe, which I kept razor-sharp, and a shovel that I made out of a dead tamarack tree that was dried hard as iron. I used it to make a ditch under the fence so the water from the little spring ran in and out of the corral around one of the rocks. Makin' the gate took some time. I made it in two pieces by usin' the wire I'd brought from the old trapper's cabin. When I got it finished it was good and stout but light enough so I could handle it quick enough to keep the horses from chargin' back out before I got it closed. I fixed up some loose poles to strengthen it and make it too high to jump.

"When it was finished I climbed back up the trail and looked it over. I was ready and it was time. I was down to eatin' venison, licorice root that I dug on a slide-rock slope, and watercress. The coffee was about gone and I was a long way from flour. There was some tea left, but it was not my favourite drink.

"Come mornin' the sun was lightin' up the peaks in rose and gold when I come to that barrier I'd built across the trail. I'd left the mare tied on the far side of the creek, where she was tellin' the world she didn't like bein' left alone. There was no horse tracks. Circlin' high I rode up into the basin and there on the far side was the horses takin' a nap in the early sun. When I got on the far slope above 'em, they still hadn't spotted me. So I rode out of sight of 'em into a twisted draw and then straight down toward 'em. When we came out of it, we were behind 'em and Ol' Baldy had 'em spotted. We was still about three hundred yards away when that mare threw up her head and let out a snort. In one jump we was all flyin' like we was a long way from home and late for breakfast. It wasn't long before that mare was headin' down the trail toward the cliff. That gimpy front shoulder didn't slow her up. When they come to the ledge they slowed up some, but you could tell she was bent on gettin' back to the big timber. When the bunch hit the bottom I wasn't far behind and they was in the trap before they even saw it. The black stud spun on his heels and charged back toward the gate but I give a war whoop and flagged him with my slicker to turn him back. I got the gate closed and wired shut and the poles fastened in place.

"Steppin' up in my saddle I got my rope ready and walked my horse slow out into the middle of the corral. The stud was frantic, all sweaty and lookin' for a hole. Then with a squeal, he charged again. My horse stepped sideways and I spread a loop on edge right under his nose. He put both front feet in it. I jerked up the slack, closin' the loop, took my dallies and spilled him tail over teakettle flat on his back. He was bawlin' like a wounded grizzly, kickin' and fightin'. Tyin' my rope on the saddle-horn, I hit the ground with a pair of good stout hobbles in my hand. He'd kicked a hind foot through between his front legs above the loop, so it was easy to buckle on the hobbles. Gettin' a short tie-rope off my saddle I tied up the hind foot with slack enough so he could get up."

Ralph reached for his cup and filled it with coffee from the pot sitting on a flat rock close to the fire. He sat there quiet for a while looking out from under the brim of his hat at the peaks that loomed down the valley under the stars, no doubt thinking of the time when he and the black stud with its spectacular white mane and tail shared a camp.

Ralph was a deeply romantic type. There was no doubt in my mind that he had been in love with the wild stallion from the time he had laid eyes on him and the memory was still vivid. I was just as sure that his captive was very lucky indeed, for Ralph had pure magic when it came to taming horses. It is a gift that few men enjoy, something that was in his make-up from birth – a kind of rapport established at first touch. The reaction with every horse is different, but the deep current of the connection is always present. It might take a great deal of patience to bring it to fruition, but given the time it will always bloom and from then on that horse will be as one with its rider.

Ralph went on to tell me that he started to handle the stud next morning by the usual method of tying up a hind foot to a loose loop around the base of the neck so he couldn't kick. As usual, the stud fought hard, but because he was young, it wasn't long before he realized he was helpless. Wringing wet with sweat and trembling he stood listening to that crooning voice and feeling the gentle stroking of a hand on his neck. Then the man began gently grooming some tangles out of the mane and tail. That soft voice scarcely ever paused all the while. Once after he got his breath back, the stallion suddenly swung his head to grab for the man's arm with his teeth, but his jaws snapped shut on nothing, while the soft cadence of the man's voice never broke its rhythm.

A horse tamer that knows the art reads a horse's intentions by watching its eyes, but Ralph was having trouble with those glass eyes that did not telegraph like normal ones. They were fiercely expressionless by comparison, so the man had to be extra careful and very patient. When the horse showed signs of sulking, he stood back, letting him have time to think things over, for by then Ralph knew the stud was intelligent.

By evening he was handling the young stud all over, and when he stood quietly without flinching when Ralph ran his hand down the middle of his back from neck to tail, and then chewed as though thinking about something to eat, Ralph took the tie-rope off his hind foot. Going out of the corral he gathered several armloads of grass.

Next day it was more of the same, but this time Ralph used only his lariat with the loop set up close behind the horse's ears for control. He named the horse Chief, and by evening the animal was following him on a slack rope around the corral.

Next morning he fitted his hackamore on the horse, then hobbled him and again tied the near hind foot up to the shoulder. Then he proceeded to saddle him. Tightening the cinch triggered some attempted bucking, but Chief soon settled down. Removing the hobbles and tie-rope, Ralph quietly led the horse around the corral. When he stopped, Chief put his nose up close to his chest and gently nuzzled his shirt.

"I went and got him some more grass and left him alone, while I chawed some jerky. Then I went back into the corral with him and he turned to face me and when I spoke to him he walked up to me. I gathered up the Macarty rope and eased up on his back.

"For a while he just stood, not moving a muscle, but when I pulled on the shank to turn him around, he bogged his head and went to bucking. It was like settin' on a big cat. He went high and crooked but he came down easy and I didn't have no trouble settin' on him. To tell the truth I was enjoyin' lookin' through that mane that was flyin' like a flag back of those black ears. He was plenty strong. He circled the corral a couple of times. Then he cut straight across towards the water. I was all set for him to hit the fence when he tried to turn. His front feet slipped and he slammed head-first into a boulder. He backed up with his head down and then he fell on his side. I come off him on to my feet as he fell and stood there lookin' at him shiver a bit and then the life just went out of him and he was dead.

"For a bit I just couldn't believe it. Then I took his head in my arms and called him. He didn't move. I don't know how long I just sat there holdin' his head, but I was cryin' like a kid. When I finally took my saddle off him, I was movin' like somebody half-dead. Without even thinkin' I went and got my horses saddled up and packed the camp to head out.

"It was night and the mountains were all lit up under a full moon, when me and the horses topped out on the pass. Lookin' ahead I could see all the way to the Lizard Range miles to the east with what was left of the old snow shinin' in the moonlight. Back of me was the valley where Chief lay dead by the spring. A rock rattled and the ol' lame mare came up beside us with her colts to stand for a while. Then she moved on down the trail and me and my horses fell in behind her."

For a while Ralph just sat with his eyes hidden behind the brim of his hat saying nothing. Then he came to his feet and looked squarely at me.

"If I could make a wish and have it come true," he said, "I would say that I wish I had never throwed a rope on him. He was too much horse to die like that!"

THE END